Soul F

MW01278557

Vegan Meals For The Health Conscience Family

Introduction

When I came to the realization that I wanted to provide a better way of health for my family than what we had been experiencing, I knew I needed to stop serving processed foods and animal based products. I did not know where to start. I felt lost and alone. Over the past 6 years I have learned how to serve delicious healthy meals. I wanted to write this book as a guide for anyone who wants to make this change and experience success. My heart for you is that you will discover that vegan meals taste good, that eating healthy does not have to be overly time consuming or costly, and that you do not have to be an expert chef to achieve this. This cookbook will give you delicious meals that you and your family will love. My hope is when you gather around the table that you will share not only the events of the day with one another but the love that comes from preparing and eating a healthy meal to feed the body and soul.

Blessings from my kitchen to yours,

Allison Adams

Over the past 16 years, I have been enjoying eating as a vegan. I changed my eating habits when I learned that I had a food allergy to milk. After eliminating milk, my skin condition improved dramatically and my ulcer related issues vanished. I love that my health and the health of my family improved by what we chose to eat. These results are also attributed to the removal of GMO's and processed foods that are loaded with toxins. To my surprise, eating vegan and organic has satisfied many of my food cravings while still feeding my body's cells. I believe these recipes are creative, delicious, and will truly satisfy your soul!

Blessings on your journey to health,

Kristen Scaife

A Review of "Soul Food", and an endorsement for healthy eating and being vegan

As diseases and sicknesses press in, making life unpleasant and difficult, many of us begin to wonder 'why'. Why are we so sick? Then, soon the 'why' grows into a search to find a way to prevent diseases in the first place. The 'why' also leads us to find ways that will help strengthen our bodies against any unwanted sickness that may come our way. Most of us who have endeavored in such a journey as this, have found that many of our problems stem from the quality of food we consume. Today with convenience always at the forefront of people's minds, many foods have been created that are actually keeping us from optimum health. In our quest, we have found that the cleaner and purer the food, the better it is for us. And we have also experienced that our bodies function much better when we stay away from animal products and by products. Soul Food is a healthy cookbook, with delicious recipes that can help us reach a fuller and more enjoyable physical life. With its unique approach, one may find a new dimension to cooking never seen before.

Yolanda Elder

Endorsement

I wish I could give a copy of this cookbook to everyone I know! When I first began my journey toward a healthier lifestyle, Allison came alongside me and helped me begin to understand what my body needed from food. She began to bring me samples of her many meals, salads, and desserts. I was shocked by how delicious they tasted!!! I kept asking, "How can this be vegan?" Even my (often discouragingly picky) children loved the food. Whenever I'd share one of Allison's meals with a group of people, I could be certain I would receive many requests for the recipe! Aside from being delicious, the meals were easy to make and didn't require unreasonable amounts of time spent in the kitchen. The ingredients were real food items that were easy to find. The food felt good to my body, mind, and spirit and left me feeling satisfied, strong, and healthy. The meals accommodated the food sensitivities of my family and provided our bodies with the nourishment they needed to heal. While it can be difficult and expensive to change eating habits, I have found these recipes to be affordable and worth the time and every penny!

Heather Shawk

Soul Food Table of Contents

Salads and Sides.. **55**

Desserts **80**

Snacks 108

Breads 112

Sauces and Dressings 117

Seasonings and Miscellaneous 123

Guidelines to read before using this book

- We use only organic ingredients. If you do not currently buy organic, we would encourage you to start with the Dirty Dozen list. The Environmental Working Group (EWG) compiles this list every year. The list contains the top 12 fruits and veggies it believes have the most residues from pesticides.
- Use distilled water for cooking if you do not have access to a good water filtration system. If you have well water, and feel it has been safely tested, that would be a good choice as well.
- When cooking, we recommend to sauté your foods with water or vegetable broth. Oils that are stable for cooking contain saturated fat, like coconut oil, which is bad for heart health (Campbell). Oils with better fats, like olive oil, will not hold up under high heat. We prefer first cold pressed extra virgin olive oil for cold recipes or slightly warm foods. Olive oil that rises close to 200° or reaches it's smoke point is to be avoided. You will see in some of our cooked recipes that contain oil; the oil is always added after the food is removed from the heat source. Check out California Olive Ranch ® at: www.californiaoliveranch.com. If you are oil free for health reasons, we have many recipes to choose from. For salads, you can

use our oil free kale salad dressing or your own favorite. Check out www.nutritionstudies.org for more information on this and other truths on how to eat healthy, founded by T. Colin Campbell.

- Parchment paper should be unbleached. Your local health food store should carry it.
- Cookware should be food grade stainless steel, cast iron, glass, or non-coated ceramic. We never use non-stick cookware. The coating releases chemicals into your food.
- The only gluten flour we use is whole-wheat einkorn. It is often referred to as the "ancient grain". It is not hybridized like all the other wheat. It has 14 chromosomes as opposed to 42 found in other wheat. Our bodies can digest einkorn well. If you have celiac disease or any wheat sensitivities, please contact your doctor before trying this gluten grain. If you substitute other flours in our recipes, the amount and baking times will change. The all-purpose einkorn flour bakes very differently and cannot be substituted equally in recipes. The germ and bran are taken out of the grain, becoming more processed. The whole-wheat flour is healthier and therefore is the only one we use. We prefer to buy einkorn products from Jovial ®. You can also purchase the whole-wheat berries for making your own flour if you have a mill. Jovial ® also offers sprouted whole-wheat einkorn flour. Check out the book:

<u>Ancient Einkorn Today's Staff of Life</u> by D. Gary Young.

- We use our homemade einkorn bread for breadcrumbs but you can use your favorite brand for our recipes if you choose not to make your own.
- The most nutrient dense salt is Himalayan salt. It has 80+ trace minerals. The second best is Celtic sea salt with over 50 trace minerals. When we use salt in our recipes, we are referring to these. We prefer to stay away from iodized table salt. People who are salt free by choice or have blood pressure issues should just exclude it.
- We prefer the high-powered Vitamix ® blender when preparing our foods. Other high power blenders can work with all our recipes as well. For chopping items such as nuts, beans, and other mixtures, a food processor will come in handy. You can still use your Vitamix ® or high-powered blender, but you may have to blend a little bit at a time.
- We prefer organic brown rice from Lundberg ® farms in California. Rice from California and Asia has the lowest levels of arsenic. Lundberg ® tests their rice and publishes their reports for the public. Inorganic arsenic is found naturally in our soil. The FDA continues to test and establish guidelines for safety. Check out Lundberg farms website and decide the right choice for you.
- You will never see soy, corn, mushrooms, or peanuts in our recipes. Soy is a

phytoestrogen, which has been labeled as an endocrine disruptor. One such source is from the Journal of Pediatric Endocrinology and Metabolism, 2010 Sep, 23(9). The research article found some benefits of soy. They also state that over a lifetime of consuming soy, findings are associated with formation of malignancies and several anomalies of the reproductive systems. Other sources will tout only the benefits. Because of these inconsistencies, we feel it is not worth the risk and choose to exclude it from our diet. Most corn is genetically modified and carries mold. Mushrooms contain mold as well. Peanuts are also high in mold and contain harmful aflatoxins. The China Study by T. Colin Campbell and Thomas M. Campbell contains information on corn, peanuts, and mold and is a wealth of health information.

- We never use processed yeast. Some information out there talks about the benefits of nutritional yeast. We do need good yeast for the health of our gut so we choose to drink homemade kombucha tea before every meal to provide that good yeast and bacteria. It is easy to make and helps balance the gut. You can research it for yourself or pick a bottle up at your local grocery and see how it makes you feel.
- We like to use natural sweeteners such as honey, black strap molasses, and maple syrup but even these should be used sparingly. Keeping this in mind, we know that a true vegan does not use honey. We

choose to use it for a sweetener because it contains natural enzymes and has 40% fruit sugar. If you are a vegan and you do not use honey, just substitute maple syrup for where you see honey in our recipes.

- For some of our desserts, we use coconut sugar. It is a natural sugar from the sap of the coconut plant. The sap is heated and after the water evaporates, the sugar is what remains. It is slightly less refined, has some nutrients, and some reports say it does not spike your blood sugar as much as regular cane sugar but we have not seen a large study to confirm this. Again, it is still sugar and treats should be used sparingly. If you want to stay away from sweeteners in foods, just eliminate them from our handful of recipes that contain it and skip our desserts.

- Ceylon cinnamon is a healthy cinnamon and has a rich flavor. Some sources say the other types of cinnamon are harmful to your health. Research for yourself and decide.

- We prefer Bob's Red Mill ® products. One of their products we use is their baking soda. They have a commitment to non-GMO and their soda is mined pure directly from the ground in its natural state. Baking soda can be mined in such a way that creates a chemical reaction and puts it through a heating process that changes it into an unnatural state.

- We have included a homemade corn free baking powder recipe in the "Seasonings and Miscellaneous" section. We have found that the homemade recipe does not get the rising action as well as the store bought kind. We have made our recipes with store bought non-GMO, aluminum free baking powder. This does however have corn in it. This is the one item in our recipes with corn but we wanted to give you a corn free alternative. If you want to use our corn free recipe, you will have to use more than what the recipe calls for to get the same rise.

- We prefer making our own egg replacer. Please see our simple and quick egg replacer recipe. It is pure and does not contain any artificial ingredients. It makes your bakery nice and fluffy.
- For a soy sauce substitute, we use coconut aminos. We prefer Coconut Secret's. If your local health food store does not have it, Amazon does. This coconut aminos has the lowest sugar and sodium content to date.
- Whenever we list something to buy that is in a can, we always look at the ingredient list. It has to be free of sugar (with a rare exception such as a can of cranberries as we have not found a juice sweetened brand). It has to have whole, organic, real food ingredients. If we do not know what we are reading, we do not buy it. Make sure the can is BPA free.
- For pasta we use whole-wheat einkorn, brown rice, or noodles made from spaghetti squash or zucchini. See directions in the

"Seasonings and Miscellaneous" section for zucchini and spaghetti squash pasta.

- When cooking with beans in our recipes, always drain the canned beans as well as your home cooked beans, except for black when directed. We use some of the bean broth from the black beans to keep them moist and add taste to our recipes.
- When using coconut milk in our desserts, shop for the brand that has the fullest fat content. Lower fat or lite products will produce a runny cream and ruin the recipe. If it is not available in your area, look for the one with the largest percentage of fat. Yes we know it has saturated fat but it is less than coconut oil and these dessert recipes should be used sparingly anyway.
- For a substitute for corn chips, we use bean chips. We prefer Beanitos ™ brand. These chips contain real ingredients and they taste wonderful.
- We love raw carob powder in some of our recipes for a cocoa replacement. It is rich in vitamins and minerals, particularly calcium. It is hard to find raw carob powder in local stores. You can purchase this item through Halleluiah Acres website by going to www.myhdiet.com. You can always buy roasted carob if you choose. We recommend purchasing the best, organic, minimally processed carob available.
- When we use canned tomatoes in our recipes, we use the entire contents in the can, juice and all. Make sure it is BPA free.

- When we list vegenaise in our recipes, we prefer to use the soy free version from the company Follow Your Heart ®.
- When using chocolate chips or melted chocolate we prefer using Enjoy Life ®. They are a great company that produces products free from the top eight allergens. This delicious chocolate only has three ingredients.
- We use Young Living Essential Oils ™ for wellness and cooking. They really enhance our lives as well as our kitchen.
- You can contact us via our website at: www.soulfood2luv.weebly.com

Fermentation Guidelines

Fermenting foods such as grains, beans, nuts, and seeds will break down the phytic acid that block nutrients from being absorbed in your body. It also aids in digestion. Fermentation is easy to do. You will need to plan 12 hours ahead or the night before. If you want to skip this step you can do so. We include canned and fermented quantities in all of our recipes. If you find that you have fermented more than you need for your recipe, freeze leftovers for later recipes in measured quantities. Ferment at room temperature. Keep in mind that there are many different variations out there for fermenting. Some individuals may find they need more fermentation time than others. Try and see what works for you.

For rice, quinoa, buckwheat, oats, millet, and all other grains including gluten:

> Soak in distilled water (it has to be non-chlorinated) for 12 hours in an acid medium.
>
> Acid includes: apple cider vinegar and lemon
>
> Ratio: 1 T. of acidic medium per 1 c. of food

For legumes:

> Soak in distilled water with an acidic medium. Soak for a minimum of 7 hours or overnight. Larger beans require a longer soaking time, from 12-24 hours.

For lentils and split peas:
>Soak for 7 hours with water only.

For nuts and seeds:
>Place the food in a bowl. Sprinkle salt over your food.
>Ratio: 1 tablespoon per 4 cups of food.
>Soak for 8 hours for smaller nuts and 12 hours for larger nuts. You can air dry them, dehydrate them, or dry in a warm oven at 170°. Use immediately or store in the fridge.

Tips:

- Allow enough water for expansion of foods, especially beans.
- Always drain and rinse food after soaking.
- Use glass bowls.
- When using nuts in recipes, if they do not need to dry, just use immediately after fermentation is done.

References: healingnaturallybybee.com, phyticacid.org

Main Dishes

The Atomic Burger

Ingredients:

1 medium onion
2 15-ounce cans of black beans, drained or 4 c.
black beans, fermented if preferred, cooked and
drained
½ c. sweet potato, cooked and peeled
½ c. walnuts, fermented if preferred
⅔ c. ground flax
2 t. chili powder
1 t. paprika
¼ c. hot sauce
½ t. salt
Sauce: vegenaise and hot sauce to taste

In a large bowl, add ground flax, paprika, chili
powder, and salt. Mix well. Chop onion in a high-
powered blender or food processor. Add the onion
to the seasoning mixture. Add remaining
ingredients in the blender or food processor and
blend well. If you are using your blender, you may
have to do the ingredients in stages for it to blend
well. Make sure there are some chunks of beans
remaining. You do not want to puree it. Pour all
the remaining blended ingredients in the large
bowl and hand mix. Form into patties. Bake on
parchment paper at 350° for 45 minutes until they
form a slight crust on top. Store on parchment
paper so they do not stick together. Mix
vegenaise and hot sauce in the amounts to your
liking in a bowl. Top the burger with the hot
sauce mixture before serving. Makes 10 burgers.

Avocado Spread Sandwich

Ingredients:

1-2 avocados (depending on the size of your bread and how thick you layer up your sandwich), peeled and thinly sliced right before eating
½ c. vegenaise
1 t. onion granules
½ t. parsley
¼ t. basil
⅛ t. thyme
A pinch of salt

Mix vegenaise, salt, and herbs in a medium size bowl until evenly mixed. Spread the veganaise mixture on both slices of bread. Thinly slice the avocado and put on top of the mixture. Spread any additional vegenaise mixture on top of the avocado if more is desired. Serve immediately. If the avocado sits too long, it will turn brown and alter the taste of this delicious sandwich.

Serves: 4

Best Pasta Sauce Ever

Ingredients:

24 ounces of pasta of choice (2 boxes)
3 15-ounce cans of chopped tomatoes
2 15-ounce cans of tomato sauce
1 large onion, chopped
6 garlic cloves, minced
2 small carrots, finely chopped
½ green pepper, finely chopped
1 small yellow squash, finely chopped
1 T. thyme
1 T. rosemary
1 T. oregano
1 T. basil
½ t. savory
2 t. salt
2 bay leaves

In a large pot, sauté onions, garlic, carrot, pepper, and squash in one tablespoon of water or broth until the vegetables soften. Add the rest of the ingredients. Bring to a boil. Cover and simmer for 30 minutes. Remove bay leaves. Serve over cooked pasta. If you want to cut the pasta in half and freeze half the sauce for a later meal, this will serve four.

Serves: 8

Note: Inspired by Yolanda, a friend of Kristen's.

Black Bean Sweet Potato Burrito

Ingredients:

6 large tortillas (store bought sprouted or our homemade oil free tortilla wraps in the "Bread" section are recommended) Note: Our homemade wraps are smaller than the larger store bought ones. You will have to make more burritos with smaller quantities of ingredients inside if you use our recipe.

4 c. cooked sweet potato, peeled and diced in half inch chunks
½ c. onion, chopped
1 garlic clove, minced
2 T. honey
1 t. maple syrup
1 15-ounce can of black beans or 2 c. black beans, fermented if preferred, and cooked
1 t. ground cumin
½ t. ground coriander
½ t. mustard powder
1 t. salt
⅛ t. ground ginger
⅛ t. ground cinnamon
Pinch of cayenne
One jar of salsa, any size
Vegenaise

Cover the potatoes with cold water in a pot and cook on high for 15-17 minutes. Do not use a lid while cooking the potatoes. Cooking time is from cold water to boiling, not 15-17 minutes of boiling. Remove from heat and drain. You should be able to stick a fork in them. Test them as you cook them. You do not want mashed sweet potatoes. While the above is cooking, add the beans to a medium size pot with the broth from the can if using canned beans. If you are cooking your own beans, use ⅓ cup of black bean broth from your cooking water. Add the spices to the beans. Mix well and heat thoroughly. Set aside and cover to keep warm. In a large skillet, sauté the garlic and onion in one tablespoon of water until they are translucent. Add the sweet potato, honey, and maple syrup. Continue to sauté this mixture for five more minutes, stirring constantly. Add small amounts of water to prevent sticking if needed. Add the bean mixture to the sweet potato mixture in the skillet. Mix well. Add mixture to a burrito wrap. Top with vegenaise and salsa before folding.

Makes 5-6 large burritos

Breakfast Burrito

Ingredients:

10 large tortillas (store bought sprouted or our homemade oil free tortilla wraps in the "Bread" section are recommended) Note: Our homemade wraps are smaller. You will have to make more burritos with smaller quantities of ingredients inside

Black Bean mixture
1 15-ounce can of black beans or 2 c. black beans, fermented if preferred, and cooked
1 t. onion powder
1 t. garlic powder
½ t. cumin
4 t. hot sauce

Potato mixture
4 medium potatoes, washed and diced in ½ to ¾ inch chunks with skins on
1 medium onion, chopped
2 t. onion powder
1 T. dried parsley
½ t. crushed rosemary
½ t. turmeric
½ t. salt

Vegenaise
One jar of salsa
Optional: green onions, olives, and jalapenos

Cover the potatoes with cold water in a pot and cook on high for 25 minutes. Do not use a lid while cooking the potatoes. When it boils, reduce to a gentle boil. Remove from heat and drain after 25 minutes is up (this is from cold water to gentle boil, not 25 minutes of boiling). Cooking times may vary. You should be able to stick a fork in them easily. Test them as you cook them. You do not want mashed potatoes. Meanwhile, add the black bean mixture ingredients to a small skillet with the broth from the can, if using canned beans. If you are cooking your own beans, use ⅓ cup of black bean broth from your cooking water. Mix well and heat through. Cover and keep warm. Once the potatoes are done, drain them. Set aside. In a large pot, put the chopped onion in one tablespoon of water. Sauté them until they become translucent. Add the potatoes and the rest of the potato mixture ingredients to the large pot. Gently stir until thoroughly mixed and potatoes start to turn brown. Layer the potato and bean mixture on your tortillas. Top with a dollop of vegenaise and salsa and any other toppings you choose. Serve immediately.

Makes 8-10 burritos

Brown Rice Bowl

Ingredients:

1½ c. uncooked brown rice, fermented if you choose
1 large red or yellow onion cut in thin strips
1 large green pepper cut in thin strips
1 c. of broccoli, cut into small pieces
4-5 garlic cloves, minced
2 medium red potatoes with the skins, baked and cut in chunks
1 15-ounce can of seasoned chopped tomatoes
1 15-ounce can black olives, sliced
Juice from one lime
Optional: 1 fresh artichoke, chopped
1 t. ground mustard
1 t. onion granules
1 t. oregano
1 t. basil
1 t. garlic granules
1 t. cumin
1 t. thyme
1 t. rosemary
1 t. marjoram
½ t. coriander
½ t. celery seed

Fry the rice in ¼ cup of water or broth for 5 minutes, stirring frequently. If you want to fry the rice a little longer, it will take about ⅓ cup. Just watch that the water does not completely evaporate so the rice will not stick to the pan. Then cook the rice according to the package directions. Add about ¾ teaspoon of salt and juice from one lime to the rice and mix well before bringing to a boil. In a large pot, sauté onion, pepper, broccoli, and garlic in one tablespoon of water or broth until softened. Remember to add the fresh artichoke in the stir-fry if you are including it in the recipe. Measure out the spices in a sealed container and shake well. Pour the spices over the sautéed vegetables. Gently fold in the potatoes. Place the rice in your serving bowls. Layer the sautéed mixture on top of the rice. Top with tomato and olives. Serve.

Tip: If cooking for later, just mix all the ingredients together in a large baking dish or pot. Bake in the oven at 350° until heated through.

Tip: You can use bean chips for dipping.

Cabbage Veggie Rice Wraps

Ingredients:

One package of spring roll rice wraps
One head of green cabbage, chopped
2 c. frozen peas
3 carrots, finely chopped
1 medium onion, chopped
3 green onions, chopped
2 t. curry
2 T. coconut aminos
1 t. salt
A pinch of cayenne

Sauté the cabbage, carrots, peas, and onions in a large pot uncovered on medium heat in ½ cup of water or broth. Stir frequently to allow everything to cook. This takes about 15 minutes. Add the spices, coconut aminos, and salt. Mix well and stir frequently for five more minutes. You want the vegetables to be tender. Prepare the wraps according to package directions. Spoon some of the mixture in the center. Wrap up ends and serve.

Serves: 8

Tip: You can exclude the rice wraps and just put it on your plate by itself if you choose.

Cauliflower Pesto Casserole

Ingredients:

1 large head of cauliflower
1 pint of cherry tomatoes, halved
5 garlic cloves, minced

Pesto:
4 ounces of fresh basil, de-stemmed and rinsed
1¼ c. olive oil
½ c. almonds, fermented if preferred
1 T. lemon juice, fresh is preferred
Salt and pepper to taste

Almond Crumbs:
1 c. breadcrumbs
1 c. almonds, fermented and dried if preferred
3 t. sage
3 t. marjoram
3 t. thyme
½ t. salt

Blend all the ingredients for the pesto sauce in a high-powered blender. Set aside. Put all the almond crumb ingredients, except for the breadcrumbs, in a high-powered blender and blend well. There should be no big almond chunks left. Add the breadcrumbs to the blender and mix well. Set aside. Cut the cauliflower into bite size florets. Place the cauliflower and garlic in a large skillet. Top with the tomatoes (you do not want them on the bottom of the skillet). The tomatoes will release enough water to soften the

food. Cook on medium until you hear a sizzle.
Then simmer covered for 15 minutes, or until the
cauliflower is al dente. Drain the cauliflower
mixture to get rid of any water. Put the mixture
back in the skillet. Remove from heat and pour
the pesto sauce over top. Mix well. Pour the
almond crumbs evenly over top. Serve
immediately.

Serves: 5-6

Chickpea Salad

Ingredients:

2 15-ounce cans of chickpeas or 4 c. chickpeas,
fermented if preferred, cooked
1 small onion, chopped
1 stalk of celery, finely chopped
1 c. vegenaise
1 t. yellow mustard
4 t. honey
1 c. bread and butter pickles, chopped
4 t. pickle juice
⅛ t. of salt
½ t. celery seed

Place the chickpeas in a high-powered blender or
food processor. The food processor works best
with this but if you do not have one, you may have
to do the ingredients in stages for it to blend well
or add some of the wet ingredients with it. Blend
until you get a "crumbled look". You do not want
pureed chickpeas. Mix all the other ingredients in
a large bowl until blended well. Add the
chickpeas and stir until they are evenly
distributed. Put on toasted bread or a romaine
lettuce leaf to serve.

Serves: 4

Creamy Ratatouille

Ingredients:

1 large onion, chopped
2 yellow, orange, or red bell peppers, chopped in small pieces
4-5 cloves of garlic, minced
4 medium zucchinis, thinly sliced
2 15-ounce cans of diced tomatoes
1 t. dried basil
½ t. oregano
1 T. dried parsley
½ t. thyme
½ t. marjoram
1 bay leaf
½ t. salt
Cashew cheese (see recipe in "Seasonings and Miscellaneous")
1 15-ounce can of black olives, sliced

Sauté onions and garlic in one tablespoon of water in a large cooking pot over medium heat. Add bell peppers and zucchini. Sauté the vegetables until they are tender, about 5-7 minutes. Add all the other ingredients except for the cashew cheese and black olives. Cover and cook for 15-20 minutes on low heat. Remove the bay leaf. Mix in the cashew cheese and black olives. Cook for an additional five minutes. Serve immediately.

Serves: 4-6

Enchiladas with Avocado Cream Sauce

Ingredients:

8 large tortillas (store bought sprouted or our homemade oil free tortilla wraps in the "Bread" section are recommended) Note: Our homemade wraps are smaller in size. You will have to make more enchiladas with smaller quantities of ingredients inside if you use our recipe

Enchilada mixture
1 15-ounce can of black beans or 2 c. black beans, fermented if desired, cooked, and drained
1 c. quinoa, fermented if desired, cooked and drained
1c. salsa
4 oz. of green chilies
1 green pepper, finely chopped
1 medium onion, chopped
5 garlic cloves, minced
1 15-ounce can of black olives, sliced
1 t. chili powder
1 t. oregano
1 t. onion granules
1 t. cumin
½ t. salt

Cream Sauce
1 avocado, peeled and deseeded
1 T. of freshly squeezed lime juice
¼ c. fresh cilantro
½ t. garlic granules
¼ t. cumin

½ t. chili powder
A big pinch of cayenne
⅛ t. salt
Black pepper to taste
⅓ c. vegenaise

Topping: A bunch of green onions, chopped

In a large skillet, sauté onion, garlic, and pepper in one tablespoon of water for 4-5 minutes. Stir in green chilies and sauté for another minute. Reduce heat to simmer. Add all the rest of the enchilada ingredients except the black olives and stir well. Fold in the olives. Cover and heat thoroughly for about 5 more minutes. Put mixture in center of tortilla wraps. Roll up the wraps and place in a covered casserole dish. Bake for 10 minutes at 350°. Meanwhile, puree the lime juice, avocado, cilantro, salt, and herbs in a high-powered blender. Place the cream sauce in a medium size bowl and fold in the vegenaise. Spoon over top of the baked enchiladas and top with the green onions. Serve immediately.

Makes 8 large enchiladas.

Tip: If the sauce is not served fresh, it will turn and not taste well.

Gingerbread Pancakes

Ingredients:

2½ c. whole-wheat einkorn flour
4 t. baking powder
1 t. baking soda
4 t. Ceylon cinnamon
1 ½ t. ginger
¼ c. blackstrap molasses
2 c. unsweetened almond milk (a slight amount more if you desire thinner batter)
½ c. egg replacer (see recipe in "Seasonings and Miscellaneous")
100% pure maple syrup

Measure dry ingredients in a large bowl. Stir to mix thoroughly. Add milk, molasses, and egg replacer. Mix well. Preheat oven to 350° and place your empty baking sheet in the oven for approximately five minutes (longer if it is a stone) before baking your pancakes. Remove from the oven and pour enough batter out to make 4-inch pancakes. Place in the center of your oven at 350° for about 12 minutes. Using a spatula, gently loosen the pancakes while holding on to the parchment paper edge for stability. Remove them with your spatula onto individual pieces of parchment paper to cool. You can stack them this way on top of each other between parchment papers to keep them from sticking and to keep warm before serving. You can reuse the same parchment paper on your baking sheet until all your pancakes are baked. The bottoms of the pancakes will be slightly ripped up but they do hold up well and this option is a healthy oil free way to eat them. Top with maple syrup.

Tip: We love this served with our cranberry orange walnut salad.

Tip: Top with hot or cold homemade applesauce (see our recipe in "Salads and Sides"), smashed berries or juice-sweetened jelly in place of maple syrup for a lower sugar option.

Tip: They fry up well in oil on a skillet if you choose just like any pancake recipe.

Makes about 25 pancakes.

Gourmet Nachos

Ingredients:

½ c. onion, diced
4 garlic cloves, minced
2 c. dry brown rice, fermented if you choose
2 T. sage
1 T. thyme
1 t. oregano
1 T. chili powder
1 T. cumin
1 t. coriander
1 t. parsley
1½ t. onion granules
2 T. coconut aminos
Two bags of bean chips

Toppings:
1 jar of salsa, any size
1 15-ounce can of black olives
1 large bunch of green onions
1 15-ounce can of black beans or 2 cups of black beans, fermented and cooked
2-3 tomatoes, chopped
Romaine lettuce, chopped
Vegenaise
1 c. cashew cheese (add 1 T. of taco seasoning when blending cheese and reduce salt to ¼ t.)
*see recipes in "Seasonings and Miscellaneous" for cheese and seasoning

Fry the rice in ¼ cup of water or broth for 5 minutes, stirring frequently. If you want to fry the rice a little longer, it will take about ⅓ cup. Just watch that the water does not completely evaporate so the rice will not stick to the pan. Then cook the rice according to the package directions. In a skillet, sauté onion and garlic in one tablespoon of water for 3-5 minutes. Add brown rice, spices, and coconut aminos. Stir well. Cook on low-medium heat for 5-7 minutes. Warm up the beans in a medium pot using the broth from your can, if using canned beans. If you are cooking your own beans, use ⅓ cup of black bean broth from your cooking water. Layer on plates in order: chips, rice mixture, beans, and cheese. Top with tomatoes, salsa, green onions, black olives, lettuce, and vegenaise.

Serves: 4

Honey Mustard Chickpeas with Rice

Ingredients:

2 c. dry brown rice, fermented if you choose
2 15-ounce cans of chick peas or 4 c. chickpeas,
fermented and cooked
⅓ c. honey
3 T. yellow mustard
1 t. salt
1 t. curry powder
2 cans of diced tomatoes
1 medium onion, chopped
5 garlic cloves, minced

Fry the rice in ¼ cup of water or broth for 5
minutes, stirring frequently. If you want to fry the
rice a little longer, it will take about ⅓ cup. Just
watch that the water does not completely
evaporate so the rice will not stick to the pan.
Then cook the rice according to the package
directions. In a large skillet, sauté the onion and
garlic in one tablespoon of water on medium-high
heat. Add all other ingredients except for the rice.
Heat for 5 minutes on medium high, and then
simmer for another 10 minutes. Serve over rice.

Serves: 8

Note: Kristen's friend, Loretta, inspired this recipe.

Italian Pasta Toss

Ingredients:

8 oz. pasta (penne, elbow, spiral, bow-tie),
uncooked
3 Roma tomatoes, diced
1 medium onion, chopped
1 medium-large zucchini, chopped
1 large yellow pepper, cut into thin strips
5 garlic cloves, minced
1 c. frozen peas
3 t. Italian seasoning
1 t. salt

Cook pasta according to package directions and
keep warm. In a large pan, sauté onion, garlic,
zucchini, pepper, peas, seasoning, and salt for 10
minutes. The peas and zucchini will add enough
liquid to sauté the food. Add tomatoes and stir
gently for 2 more minutes. Stir in warm pasta.
Spoon your pasta into bowls.

Serves: 4

Lasagna

Ingredients:

1 package of brown rice lasagna noodles
2 15-ounce cans of tomato sauce
6-ounce can of tomato paste
1 medium zucchini, grated or your favorite
vegetable
One large bunch of fresh spinach leaves, de-
stemmed
1 large onion, chopped
2 c. cashew cheese (see recipe in "Seasonings and
Miscellaneous")
2 t. garlic granules
2 t. oregano
2 t. basil
1 t. salt

Cook noodles in boiling water with a little salt for
5 minutes. They will be stiff but will cook the rest
of the way in the oven. Drain. Separate and lay
flat on parchment paper. In a pan, sauté the
zucchini and onion in one tablespoon of water
until softened. Add tomato sauce, tomato paste,
spices, and salt. Mix well. Cook on low heat until
heated through, stirring occasionally. Spread four
tablespoons of the tomato sauce in the bottom of
a 9X13 pan. This will be just enough to wet the
bottom. Layer the pan with a layer of noodles.
Slightly overlap them to have four across and a
short one at the end. You will have one noodle
left when you are done. You can use it
somewhere in the layers if you choose. Spread

half of the tomato sauce on top of the noodles. Place half of the cheese in even dollops over the sauce. Gently spread evenly over the sauce with a spoon. Layer enough spinach to cover the cheese. Repeat the layers with the remaining ingredients. Make sure all the noodle edges are covered so they will not burn. Bake at 350° for 30 minutes. Let the lasagna sit for a few minutes before cutting.

Latkes

Ingredients:

3 medium potatoes, peeled and shredded
One medium onion, chopped
One bunch of green onions, chopped
½ c. carrot, shredded
½ c. whole-wheat einkorn flour
½ c. egg replacer (see recipe in "Seasonings and Miscellaneous")
1 t. salt
2 t. garlic granules
2 t. onion granules
1 t. paprika
½ t. dry mustard
½ t. black pepper
Barbeque sauce (see recipe in "Sauces and Dressings")

Toppings:
Applesauce (see recipe in "Salads and Sides")
Barbeque buffalo bites (see recipe in "Salads and Sides")

Grate the potatoes. Place the potatoes in a large bowl. Put the flour, spices, and salt in a separate small bowl. Mix well. Pour this flour mixture and the rest of the ingredients in with the potatoes and mix well. Shape into patties. Place on parchment paper on a cooking sheet. Bake at 350° for 45 minutes. Top half with cold applesauce and half with the warm barbeque buffalo bites. Drizzle some warm barbeque sauce

over the barbeque bite latkes. Serve immediately.
If you prefer only one topping you can choose
your favorite.

Tip: We make the whole buffalo bites recipe and
applesauce recipe and serve extras as a side dish
with this meal or you can save them for another
meal. Store bought applesauce will not taste
good on these. We also like these topped with
ketchup or vegenaise.

Makes 8 latkes

Lentil Loaf

Ingredients:

4 c. lentils, fermented if you choose, cooked
1 c. pecans, fermented if you choose
½ c. breadcrumbs
½ c. dry rolled gluten free oats, ground fine
1 large onion, chopped
3 T. coconut aminos
1 T. apple cider vinegar
3 T. sage
1 T. thyme
2 t. Italian seasoning
1 t. salt
1t. garlic granules
1 t. onion granules
1 t. mustard powder
⅓ c. ketchup
Additional ketchup for topping

Put onion in a small skillet and sauté in one tablespoon of water until softened. Put the onion and breadcrumbs in a large bowl. Blend the remaining ingredients in a high-powered blender or food processor. The food processor works best with this but if you do not have one, you may have to do the ingredients in stages for it to blend well. Keep mixture slightly chunky. Add the blended food to the onions and breadcrumbs. Hand mix well. Taking about ½ cup of the mixture, shape into ¾ inch thick rectangular patties with rounded edges so they will not burn. Put on parchment paper on a baking tray. Top with a little more ketchup and using a spoon, spread it evenly over the top for a glaze. Bake at 350° for 40 minutes. Put on toasted bread for a lentil loaf sandwich if desired or serve plain.

Makes: 12-14 loaf patties

Tip: Leftover loaves taste great as a cold sandwich with added ketchup, if desired.

Lentil Pea Soup

Ingredients:

1½ c. dried lentils, fermented if desired
2 c. split peas, fermented if desired, cooked
1 large yellow onion, finely chopped
4 medium carrots, finely chopped
2 large stalks of celery, finely chopped
8 cloves of garlic, minced
1 leek, chopped (make sure it is rinsed well as dirt tends to hide in the layers)
2 15-ounce cans of diced tomatoes
8 c. vegetable broth
2 whole bay leaves
1 T. parsley
1 T. garlic granules
1 T. onion granules
2 t. salt
2 t. basil
2 t. marjoram
2 t. cumin
2 t. turmeric
2 t. coriander seed
1 t. chili powder

In a large pot, sauté carrots, onion, celery, garlic, and leek in two tablespoons of water or broth over moderately low heat until onions are tender, about 5 minutes. Add dry lentils, tomatoes, bay leaves, broth, and spices. Bring to a boil. Reduce heat to low, cover, and cook for 40 minutes covered, or until lentils are tender. Add in the cooked split peas. Bring to a second boil and simmer again for 5 more minutes. Discard the bay leaves before serving.   Makes a 5-quart stockpot.

Minestrone Soup

Ingredients:

1 large onion
5 garlic cloves, minced
3 bay leaves
8 c. vegetable broth
1 15-ounce can chopped tomatoes
6 oz. tomato paste
2 carrots, thinly chopped
2 celery stalks, thinly chopped
1 large red potato, diced with skins on
1 15-ounce can of kidney beans or 2 c. kidney beans, fermented and cooked
1 15-ounce can of cannellini beans or 2 c. cannellini beans, fermented and cooked
1 T. basil
1 T. oregano
½ c. fresh parsley, chopped

Sauté garlic and onion in one tablespoon of water or broth in a large pot until softened. Add broth, bay leaves, tomatoes, tomato paste, carrots, celery, and potatoes. Bring to a boil, reduce heat, cover, and simmer for 50 minutes. Add dried oregano, basil, parsley, and beans. Cook the soup on medium heat for 10 minutes, or until it is thoroughly heated. Remove bay leaves just before serving.
 Makes a large 5.5-quart stockpot of soup.

Pizza

Ingredients:

Crust:
3 c whole-wheat einkorn flour
1 c. warm water
3 t. baking powder
1 T. raw unfiltered honey

1 15-ounce can of pizza sauce
Toppings of your choice (favorites of ours: red onion, pepperoncini peppers, bell peppers, black olives, tomato, pineapple, and buffalo bites *see recipe under "Salads and Sides")
1 c. cashew cheese (see recipe in "Seasonings and Miscellaneous"), add some fresh basil when blending if desired)

Mix dry crust ingredients in a bowl. Add honey and water. Stir. Knead until it forms a soft dough. Sprinkle with a dusting of flour on the dough to prevent sticking. Let rise in a glass bowl in a warm place for 30 minutes. Line your baking sheet with parchment paper to fit. Spread dough on your parchment lined baking sheet. Spread sauce on the dough. Top with your toppings of choice. Lastly, drop small dollops of cheese over it. Bake at 350° for 20-30 minutes. Cooking time will be largely based on the type of pan you use. Thinner metal pans will be done sooner while a baking stone may take longer.

Pocket Foldovers

Ingredients:

Pizza Dough:
3 c whole-wheat einkorn flour
1 c. warm water
3 t. baking powder
1 T. raw unfiltered honey

Sauce:
½ c. vegenaise
¼ c. yellow mustard

Mix well in a small bowl.

Toppings of choice:
Buffalo bites (see recipe in "Sides and Salads") *
the hot bites really make these foldovers delicious
Pepperoncini peppers
Red onion, chopped
Black olives, chopped
Roma tomato's, chopped
Pineapple, chopped

Drizzle topping:
¼ c. vegenaise
2 T. yellow mustard

Mix together in a small bowl while the foldovers
are baking.
Mix pizza dough according to directions. Divide
dough evenly into 8 balls. Dust each dough ball
lightly with flour. Place balls into bowl. Cover

and place in a 170° oven that was heated and turned off or a toaster oven on warm for 30 minutes. Take one ball out at a time making sure to keep the others covered. Generously flour the bottom of each ball. Press on parchment paper on a cooking sheet into a 6 to 6½ inch circle. Gently lift up each flattened dough piece, re-flour and reposition any needed area. Place ⅛ of the sauce into the middle of the dough. It should be a large spoonful. Top with your favorite toppings. Gently fold the dough over the ingredients making a moon shape. Seal where the dough meets with your fingers. Make sure not to over stuff these as they will create holes in the dough and the sauce will leak out when baking. After all 8 foldovers are sealed, bake at 350° for 20 minutes. When they are done baking, drizzle the topping on the foldovers and serve.

Makes 8 foldovers

Potato Chili Stew

Ingredients:

2 15-ounce cans of kidney beans or 4 c. kidney beans, fermented if preferred and cooked
1-quart tomato juice
¾ c. green pepper, chopped
1 large onion, chopped
6 medium russet potatoes, peeled and chopped in small chunks
2 medium carrots, chopped thinly

1 t. chili powder
1½ t. salt
½ t. cumin
¼ t. oregano
½ t. coriander seed
¼ t. cayenne pepper
1 t. garlic powder
1 t. onion powder
¼ t. crushed red pepper
1 T. celery seed

Put potatoes, carrots, and a teaspoon of salt into a medium pot with 5 c. of water. Bring to a boil. Reduce heat and simmer to a gentle boil uncovered for approximately 10 minutes, or until potatoes are tender. Do not drain. While waiting, sauté the peppers and the onions in one tablespoon of water or broth in a large pot until onions are translucent. Add the potato, carrot, and salted water and all other ingredients, including the 1½ t. of salt listed in the ingredients. Cover and bring to a boil, lower heat, and simmer for 15 minutes. Serve.

Makes a 5-quart stockpot of soup.

Pumpkin Chili Burger

Ingredients:

1 c. red onion, chopped
1 c. green pepper, chopped
6 garlic cloves, minced
1 15-ounce can of black beans or 2 c. black beans,
fermented if preferred, cooked and drained
1 15-ounce can of kidney beans or 2 c. kidney
beans, fermented if preferred and cooked
½ c. canned pumpkin puree
2 c. breadcrumbs
1 c. pecans, fermented if you choose, chopped
2 t. cumin
1½ t. salt

Sauté the onion, pepper, and garlic in one
tablespoon of water until the onions are soft.
Make sure the water is cooked off. Blend beans in
a high-powered blender or food processor. The
food processor works best with this but if you do
not have one, you may have to do the ingredients
in stages for it to blend well. You want the beans
to be slightly chunky. Mix all the ingredients
together in a large bowl. Form into patties. Bake
on parchment paper at 350° for 25-30 minutes
until they form a light crust on the top. Store
between parchment papers. Serve with favorite
burger toppings.

Makes 11-12 burgers.

Stuffed Peppers with Spanish Rice

Ingredients:

4 green peppers
2 c. uncooked brown rice, fermented if you choose
1 medium onion
3 garlic cloves, minced
2 15-ounce cans of diced tomatoes
1 T. honey
½ t. chili powder
½ t. salt
2 T. of hot sauce
1 15-ounce can of tomato sauce
1 t. garlic granules
1 t. oregano
1 t. basil

Fry the rice in ¼ cup of water or broth for 5 minutes, stirring frequently. If you want to fry the rice a little longer, it will take about ⅓ cup. Just watch that the water does not completely evaporate so the rice will not stick to the pan. Then cook the rice according to the package directions. In another skillet, sauté garlic and onion in one tablespoon of water until softened. Add to the cooked rice along with the diced tomatoes, honey, ½ t. salt, chili powder, and hot sauce. Stir well. Meanwhile, cut the green peppers in half long ways so that they are shaped like a boat. De-seed and remove stems. Drop into salted boiling water for 5 minutes and place in a 9X13 casserole dish. Sprinkle the bottom of each pepper with a small pinch of salt. Fill them to overflowing with the rice mixture. Mix one can of tomato sauce in a small pan with the garlic granules, oregano, and basil. Pour over the peppers. Smooth out evenly with a spoon. Pour the remaining tomato sauce over the remaining rice and keep warm on the stove. Bake the peppers uncovered at 350° for 30 minutes. Serve with a small side of the Spanish rice if desired.

Makes 8 halved peppers and extra rice for a small side dish

Sweet and Sour Stir Fry

Ingredients:

1½ c. dry brown rice, fermented if preferred
1 15-ounce can of pineapple or 2 c. fresh pineapple, diced
5 oz. can of water chestnuts, chopped
A medium bunch of fresh bok choy, chopped
10 oz. frozen or fresh sugar snap peas
2 c. fresh broccoli cut in small pieces

Sauce:
1 medium onion, finely chopped
4 cloves of garlic, minced
2 T. fresh ginger, finely grated and firmly packed to measure
2 t. hot sauce
1 c. ketchup
¼ c. and 2 T. coconut aminos
¼ c. apple cider vinegar
2 T. honey

Fry the rice in ¼ cup of water or broth for 5 minutes, stirring frequently. If you want to fry the rice a little longer, it will take about ⅓ cup. Just watch that the water does not completely evaporate so the rice will not stick to the pan. Then cook the rice according to the package directions. Meanwhile, put the onion, garlic, and ginger in a small skillet in one tablespoon of water or broth. Sauté the ingredients until softened. Add the rest of the sauce ingredients and stir over low-medium heat for 5 minutes or until the sauce thickens. Set aside. In a large skillet, put the remaining ingredients in one tablespoon of water or broth. Sauté on medium heat for 8-10 minutes. Add the rice and sauce to the skillet and mix well. Serve immediately.

Serves: 6

Sweet Beans over Rice

Ingredients:

1 ½ c. dry brown rice, fermented if you choose
2 15-ounce cans baked beans or your favorite homemade recipe
3 medium green peppers cut in strips
1 large onion, chopped
6 garlic cloves
2 T. ginger root, freshly grated and firmly packed to measure
¼ c. coconut aminos
8 oz. can of water chestnuts
A bunch of fresh bok choy, chopped
⅔ c. fresh squeezed orange juice

Fry the rice in ¼ cup of water or broth for 5 minutes, stirring frequently. If you want to fry the rice a little longer, it will take about ⅓ cup. Just watch that the water does not completely evaporate so the rice will not stick to the pan. Then cook the rice according to the package directions. Sauté onions, peppers, water chestnuts, garlic, bok choy, and ginger root in one tablespoon of water or broth in a large stockpot until the food begins to soften. Remove from heat. Add orange juice and coconut aminos and stir well. Add the cooked rice and stir well. Fold in baked beans until well blended. Serve immediately.

Serves: 8

Taco Salad with Zucchini Shells

Ingredients:

Taco Shells:
4 c. zucchini, grated and drained (measure after draining and pack tightly in measuring cup, about 4 medium zucchinis)
¼ c. egg replacer
¾ c. breadcrumbs
½ t. black pepper
½ t. salt
½ t. garlic granules
½ t. cumin
½ t. onion granules
¼ t. coriander
¼ t. chili powder

Toppings:
One 15-ounce can of black beans or 2 c. of black beans, fermented if preferred and cooked
3 T. taco seasoning (see recipe in "Seasonings and Miscellaneous")
1 15-ounce can of black olives, drained and chopped
1 jar of salsa, any size
1 large bunch of green onions, chopped
3-4 medium tomatoes
1 bunch of romaine lettuce, chopped
Vegenaise

Press grated zucchini in colander to drain excess moisture. Then measure out 4 cups packed tightly in a measuring cup. Place in a large bowl. In a small bowl or blender, mix the breadcrumbs, spices, and salt together. Add the breadcrumb mixture and egg replacer to the zucchini and stir with a large spoon finishing with kneading with your hands if needed. Place parchment paper on several baking sheets. Drop a large spoonful (about 2 tablespoons) of the mixture on the parchment paper and flatten in a circle. Bake the shells at 400° for about 30 minutes, or until it starts to brown on the edges. Turn the pans halfway through so the shells in the back of the oven will not burn. You may have to bake them longer depending on how thin or thick you flattened the shells. Try to get them as thin as possible to ensure even baking. If they start browning in the middle, you have baked them too much. Let it sit for a few minutes before peeling slowly off the paper. Serve immediately or store between parchment papers in a sealed container. Makes: 12 shells

Place beans in a pan on low heat with the broth from the can, if using canned beans. If you are cooking your own beans, use ⅓ cup of black bean broth from your cooking water. Add 3 T. of taco seasoning. Mix beans well so they are evenly seasoned and warmed through. Place the taco shell on a plate. Top with warm beans and the rest of the ingredients. Add several small dollops of vegenaise on top. Eat with a fork.

Serves: 4

Tomato Basil Pasta

Ingredients:

12oz. of pasta of choice
1 medium onion, chopped
4 garlic cloves, minced
1 pint of grape tomatoes, sliced
1½ t. onion granules
1½ t. garlic granules
1 t. salt
½ c. olive oil
¾ c. fresh basil, de-stemmed and rinsed, packed tightly for measure
¼ c. pine nuts

Cook pasta according to package directions. In a large pot, sauté onion, garlic, and tomatoes until the onions are softened. The tomatoes release enough liquid to sauté. Remove from heat. Place the basil, olive oil, salt, and garlic and onion granules in a high-powered blender and blend until chopped fine. Add cooked pasta, oil and basil mixture, and the pine nuts to the onions, garlic, and tomato mixture that are removed from the heat source. Serve immediately.

Serves: 4

White Bean Chili

Ingredients:

3 15-ounce cans northern white beans or 6 c.
northern white beans, fermented if preferred and
cooked
1 15-ounce can garbanzo beans or 2 c. garbanzo
beans, fermented if preferred and cooked
2 large onions, chopped
8 c. vegetable broth
8 ounces of green chilies
6-8 garlic cloves, minced
4 t. cumin
4 t. dried oregano
¼ t. clove
⅛ t. cayenne pepper
Vegenaise
One jar of salsa, any size

In a large pot, sauté onions and garlic in one
tablespoon of water or vegetable broth until the
onions are soft. Add green chilies, cumin,
oregano, clove, and cayenne pepper. Sauté for
one more minute. Add broth and beans. Heat on
medium until thoroughly heated, about 20
minutes. Put in bowls and top with a dollop of
vegenaise and salsa. Serve.

Makes a large 5.5-quart stockpot of soup.

Tip: The vegenaise and salsa on top really make
this dish taste gourmet.

Salads and
Sides

Almost Waldorf Salad

Ingredients:

3 crunchy eating apples any variety, chopped with skins on
1 c. red grapes, halved
½ c. pecans, fermented if preferred and dried, chopped
½ c. celery, chopped
½ c. vegenaise

Mix all the ingredients in a medium size bowl and serve. Refrigerate.

Serves: 4

Applesauce

Ingredients:

4 sweet cooking apples, peeled and chopped
Water
½ t. cinnamon
A large pinch of nutmeg

Place the apples in a medium pan with enough water to cover the bottom of the baking dish, about one-fourth to one-third cup. Cover and bring to a boil. Reduce heat and simmer for 10 minutes making sure the water does not evaporate. Add more water if needed. Add cinnamon and nutmeg. Cover again and simmer for 10 more minutes or until apples are soft. Mash

them with a fork for a chunky applesauce.
Refrigerate.

Serves: 4

Broccoli Salad

Ingredients:

8 c. of fresh broccoli florets
1 c. of raw sunflower seeds, fermented and dried if
preferred
1 c. of golden raisins
1 medium red onion, chopped
1 c. vegenaise
2 T. apple cider vinegar
¼ c. honey

Mix the vegenaise, honey, and vinegar in a large
bowl. Add the rest of the ingredients and mix
well. Serve immediately.

Tip: This side dish tastes best fresh. The
sunflower seeds will soften by the next day.

Serves: 6-8

Buffalo Bites

Ingredients:

1 large size head of cauliflower

Dipping batter:
1 c. whole-wheat einkorn flour
1½ c. unsweetened almond milk
2 t. garlic granules
3 t. onion granules
1½ t. cumin
1 t. paprika
1 t. ground mustard
¼ t. salt

In a medium bowl, combine all dry ingredients and mix well. Add the milk and stir until the batter is smooth.

Choice of two sauces:

Barbeque Sauce
1 c. barbeque sauce (see recipe in "Sauces and Dressings")

Hot sauce
½ c. hot sauce

Salt and vinegar sauce
3 T. apple cider vinegar
Salt to taste

Note: After dipping the bites into the vinegar and laying them on parchment paper, sprinkle bites with salt to taste. Pour remaining vinegar over bites.

Honey Mustard Sauce
¼ c. honey
3 T. yellow mustard

Cut the cauliflower in to small bite size florets. Dip the florets into the dipping batter and lay on baking sheets on parchment paper. Make sure they are not touching and that they are coated well. Bake at 450° for 30 minutes, after 20 minutes take them out of the oven. Using your hands or a spatula, turn them over. They should lift off very easily. Place back in the oven for the remaining 10 minutes. Choose the sauces you wish to season the bites with. Two of the sauces will be adequate for a whole head of cauliflower. If you only want one flavor, double the recipe. Remove from the oven again. Dip the baked bites into the sauce of choice and lay them back on the parchment paper. Bake for 10-15 more minutes at 450° depending on your sauce choice. The barbeque sauce is thicker and will tend to take more than 10 minutes. Serve plain or with ranch dip (see recipe in "Sauces and Dressings").

Caribbean Salad

Ingredients:

5 ounces of fresh spinach, washed
16 ounces of fresh strawberries, washed and cut up
1 10.7-ounce can of mandarin oranges, drained
1 small red onion, finely chopped
1 c. walnut pieces, fermented and dried if preferred
Poppy seed dressing (See recipe in "Sauces and Dressings") * this recipe will be more than enough for the entire salad

In a large bowl, place spinach and red onion. Mix well. Add fruits and fold in. Sprinkle the top with the walnuts. Serve and top with dressing.

Serves: 6-8 depending on if it is a side dish or a main meal

Cold Pasta Salad

Ingredients:

12 ounces of pasta of choice
1 c. of fresh or frozen peas
1 small-medium cucumber, sliced and quartered
1 pint of grape or cherry tomatoes, halved
1 15-ounce can of black olives
1¼ c. of homemade Italian Dressing (see recipe in "Sauces and Dressings")

Optional: Cashew cheese (this is slightly different from our regular version)
1 c. cashews, fermented if preferred
¼ c. water
¼ t garlic granules
1 t. onion powder
1 t lemon juice
½ t. salt
¼ c. fresh basil or more to taste, de-stemmed and rinsed, packed tightly for measure

Blend cheese ingredients in a high-powered blender until smooth.

Cook pasta according to the package directions. Let cool. Mix in all the vegetables and pour the dressing over top and mix well. Options for the cashew cheese include: adding a dollop on top of your individual serving, mixing in the cup of cheese through the entire pasta dish right before serving, or excluding the cheese and eating it plain. Refrigerate. Serves: 6-8

Cold Vegetable Pizza

Ingredients:

Crust
3 c whole-wheat einkorn flour
1 c. warm water
3 t. baking powder
1 T. raw unfiltered honey
1½ t. onion granules
1½ t. garlic granules
1 t. parsley
½ t. basil
½ t. oregano
¼ t. thyme

Cashew cheese (this is slightly different from our regular version)
1 c. cashews, fermented if preferred
¼ c. water
¼ t garlic granules
1 t. onion powder
1 t lemon juice
½ t. salt
¼ c. fresh basil or more to taste, de-stemmed and rinsed, packed tightly for measure

Blend cheese ingredients in a high-powered blender until smooth.

Ranch dressing (this is slightly different from our salad dressing)
1 c. vegenaise
2 t. onion granules

2 t. parsley
2 t. dill
2 t. chives
1 t. garlic granules
½ t. dry mustard powder
¼ t. salt

Mix all ingredients in a small bowl.

<u>Toppings</u>
½ c. red onion, chopped
1 c. cauliflower, cut into small florets
1 c. broccoli, cut into small florets
1 c. grated carrot
1 15-ounce can of black olives, sliced

Mix dry crust ingredients in a bowl. Add honey and water. Stir. Knead until it forms a soft dough. Sprinkle with a dusting of flour on the dough to prevent sticking. Let rise in a glass bowl in a warm place for 30 minutes. Line your baking sheet with parchment paper to fit. Spread dough on your parchment lined baking sheet. You may need to lightly dust the top with flour when flattening the dough with your hands. Bake at 350° for 10-15 minutes depending on the type of baking sheet you use. Remove from oven and cool. Once the crust is completely cool to the touch, spread the cashew cheese in a thin even layer over the crust. Next, spread the ranch dressing evenly over the cashew cheese. Sprinkle the onion, carrot, and olives evenly over top. Lastly, place the broccoli and cauliflower evenly over the top. Gently press on the toppings so that they will stay on the pizza better. Cover and chill in the refrigerator or serve right away.

Tip: Add additional favorite toppings including, but not limited to: tomatoes, pepperoncini peppers, green onion, and bell peppers. You may need to cut down on the quantity of other toppings depending on how much you add.

Cranberry Orange Walnut Salad

Ingredients:

One 15-ounce can of whole cranberries
2 oranges, peeled, de-skinned and de-seeded; cut in small bite size pieces
¾-1 c. of walnuts, fermented and dried if preferred, chopped

Mix all of the ingredients together and serve.

Serves: 4

Tip: You can top with whipping cream (see recipe in "Seasonings and Miscellaneous") for a treat.

Tip: You can use fresh cranberries when they are in season. Cook according to package directions and sweeten with maple syrup to taste.

Creamy Cucumber Salad

Ingredients:

1 medium red onion, diced
2 medium cucumbers, sliced half inch thick and halved
2 large tomatoes, chopped
2 T. apple cider vinegar
½ c. vegenaise
1 T. dried parsley
1 t. salt
1 t. dill

Mix cucumber, onion, and tomato and toss. Add the rest of the ingredients and mix. Refrigerate at least two hours.

Tip: If the cut of the cucumber is too thin, they will wilt and not be crunchy.

Tip: This dish is best if eaten the same day.

Serves: 4

Dilly Bean Salad

Ingredients:

2 15-ounce cans chickpeas or 4 c. chickpeas,
fermented if preferred, cooked and chilled
¼ c. and 3 T. apple cider vinegar
¼ c. and 1 T. honey
1 large cucumber, sliced in half moons or smaller
1 T. dill
Salt to taste

Mix all ingredients in a medium size bowl. Chill
and serve.

Serves: 6-8

Glazed Green Beans

Ingredients:

1 lb. of fresh green beans
1 large onion, chopped
2 garlic cloves, minced
2 T. honey
2 T. olive oil
½ t. salt

Trim and clean the green beans. Bring 6 cups of
water to a boil in a large pot. Add one teaspoon
of salt to the water. Boil the green beans for 4
minutes. Drain and shock the beans by rinsing
them with cold water. Sauté the onion and garlic
in one tablespoon of water in a large skillet until

softened. Add the beans, ½ teaspoon of salt, and honey to the skillet. Heat for one minute longer while stirring. Remove from heat and add olive oil. Mix well. Serve immediately.

Serves: 4

Tip: This recipe makes a crisper bean. If you like your beans tender, just boil or steam them until the desired tenderness is reached.

Grandma's Kidney Bean Salad

Ingredients:

1 15-ounce can of kidney beans or 2 cups of kidney beans, fermented if desired, and cooked and chilled
15 ounces of frozen or fresh peas
4 stalks of celery, chopped
1 medium onion, chopped fine
1-2 carrots, grated
¾ c. vegenaise
Salt and pepper to taste

Mix ingredients in a bowl and chill for at least 30 minutes before serving.

Serves: 4

Grandma's Potato Salad

Ingredients:

4 c. of red potatoes, peeled and diced in ½ to ¾ inch chunks
4 stalks of celery, chopped fine
¼ c. onion, chopped
1 c. vegenaise
1 T. apple cider vinegar
3 T. unsweetened almond milk
2 t. yellow mustard
1½ T. honey
½ t. celery seed
½ t. salt

Cover the potatoes with cold water in a pot and cook on high for 25 minutes. Do not use a lid while cooking the potatoes. When it boils, reduce to a gentle boil and remove from heat and drain after 25 minutes is up (this is from cold water to gentle boil, not 25 minutes of boiling). Cooking time may vary. You should be able to easily stick a fork in them. Test them as you cook them. You do not want mashed potatoes. Pour them in a large bowl and chill. Once they are cold, add the rest of the ingredients and stir. Serve immediately or refrigerate.

Serves: 8

Guacamole with Bean Chips

Ingredients:

One bag of bean chips
2 avocados, peeled and de-pitted
½ c. red onion, chopped
2 garlic cloves, minced
2 T. of fresh squeezed lime juice
½ t. cumin
¼ t. salt
2 large pinches of cayenne
Optional: Fresh tomatoes, chopped
Optional: A bunch of fresh cilantro to taste

Place the avocados, lime juice, garlic, spices, and salt in a high-powered blender. Add the cilantro at this time if you choose. Blend until smooth. Fold in the onion. Place in a medium size serving bowl and add the tomatoes if desired. Eat that same day. Refrigerate in a sealed container if you are not serving it right away.

Serves: 4

Honey Mustard Buffalo Bites over Arugula

Ingredients:

Honey mustard buffalo bites (see recipe in "Salads and Sides"), one whole recipe of honey mustard bites (you may have some left over depending on how many you want on each salad)
5-ounce tub of arugula lettuce
Half a cucumber, sliced
2-3 stalks of celery, chopped
One pint of cherry or grape tomatoes
Sunflower seeds, fermented and dried if preferred
Pecans or walnuts, fermented and dried if preferred, chopped
Alfalfa sprouts
Honey Mustard dressing (see recipe in "Sauces and Dressings") *this recipe will be enough for the entire salad

Place lettuce on the bottom of the salad bowls. Top with desired amounts of each vegetable and top with nuts and sprouts. Place buffalo bites on top, hot or cold. Pour dressing on top and serve.

Serves: 6

Hot Potato Yum

Ingredients:

7 medium potatoes with or without skins, chopped in ½ to ¾ inch pieces
5 medium carrots, sliced thinly

2 celery stalks, chopped
1 medium onion, chopped
4 garlic cloves, chopped
4 t. marjoram
¼ c. olive oil
¾ t. salt
Black pepper to taste

In a large pot, cover the potatoes and carrots with cold, lightly salted water. Cook on high for 20 minutes. Do not use a lid while cooking the potatoes. Cooking time is from cold water to boiling, not 20 minutes of boiling. Cooking times may vary. You should be able to stick a fork in them easily. Test them as you cook them. You do not want mashed potatoes. Remove from heat. Drain, cover, and set aside. In a medium skillet, sauté celery, onion and garlic in one tablespoon of water or broth. Sauté until they become transparent. Add marjoram and ¾ teaspoon of salt and sauté for another minute. Combine the sautéed mixture with the potatoes and carrots. Mix well. Remove from heat. Add ¼ c. of olive oil and black pepper to taste. Mix well. Serve immediately.

Serves: 8

Tip: If you are watching oil intake, just exclude this last step. This dish will still taste wonderful. To avoid any dryness without oil, just add a little bit of almond milk at the end.

Note: Inspired by Yolanda, a friend of Kristen's.

Kale Salad

Ingredients:

One large bunch of kale
3 large oranges
Freshly squeezed lemon juice from half of a lemon
3½ t. maple syrup
⅓ c. dried cranberries (juice sweetened, if available)
1 c. pecans, fermented if preferred
1 t. cinnamon
1 t. vanilla extract

Dressing:
2 T. fresh squeezed orange juice
1 t. Dijon mustard
2 T. apple cider vinegar
2 T. honey
2 T. olive oil

In a small bowl, add two teaspoons of the maple syrup, cinnamon, and vanilla. Mix well. Add the pecans on top and mix well. Place in a glass pan in a single layer and bake at 170° stirring occasionally until they begin to dry and the mixture crystalizes on the nuts, about 20 minutes. Set aside. If you do not ferment, the baking time will be shorter. Watch that you do not burn the nuts. Juice the lemon and one orange. Set aside two tablespoons of orange juice for the dressing. Place the remaining juice in a large bowl with 1½ teaspoons of maple syrup. Mix well. Chop the kale and place it on top of the juice mixture.

Hand massage the kale with the juice mixture until it softens the kale, usually about 2-3 minutes. Peel, cut and de-seed the remaining two oranges into bite size pieces and place in the salad. You can peel the orange skins off, if you prefer. Add the cranberries. Mix well. Add the dressing ingredients to a cruet and shake well. Place salad in bowls and top with nuts and a little bit of dressing.

Serves: 4-6

Mediterranean Salad

Ingredients:

12 ounces of romaine lettuce, washed and chopped
One 15-ounce can of black olives, chopped
2 T. pepperoncini's, drained and chopped
½ c. red onion, chopped
1 c. red cabbage, chopped
1 c. carrots, grated
One pint of grape or cherry tomatoes, halved
2 c. of croutons (see recipe in "Breads")
Italian Dressing (see recipe in "Sauces and Dressings")* you may need to double the dressing recipe depending on how much dressing you prefer

Toss the ingredients in a large bowl. Place in bowls and pour desired amount of dressing on each salad.
Serves: 6

Peasant Peas

Ingredients:

16 ounces of frozen or fresh peas
3 T. olive oil
1 T. lemon juice
1 t. honey
½ c. onion, chopped
½ t. dill
½ t. garlic granules
½ t. salt

Mix all ingredients in a medium size bowl. Serve immediately. This dish needs to be prepared and served the same day to preserve the taste.

Serves: 4-6

Seasoned Brussels Sprouts

Ingredients:

1½ pounds of Brussels sprouts (fresh is recommended)
2 T. olive oil
1 t. onion granules
1 t. parsley
½ t. cumin
½ t. curry
1½ t. salt

Rinse and trim off any bad looking outer leaves on your Brussels sprouts. Cut the bottom core off of each sprout by about ¼ inch. Then cut your Brussels sprouts into quarters or halves. Steam them for about 8 minutes or until fork tender. Do not let them get too mushy. Place the seasonings into a small sealed container and shake well to mix. Place the steamed sprouts into a medium glass bowl or dish. Toss with the seasonings and oil and serve immediately. Serves: 4-6

Spicy Buffalo Ranch Salad

Ingredients:

12 oz. of Romaine lettuce, washed and chopped
1 c. red cabbage, chopped
1 medium cucumber, chopped
1 c. carrot, chopped
½ c. slivered almonds, fermented and dried if preferred
½ c. dried, unsulfured cranberries, juice sweetened
Hot buffalo bites (see recipe in "Salads and Sides"), one whole recipe of hot buffalo bites (you may have some left over depending on how many you want on each salad)
Ranch dressing (See recipe in "Sauces and Dressings") *this recipe will be enough for the entire salad

Mix the first six ingredients in a large bowl. Place into serving salad bowls. Top with desired amount of buffalo bites, hot or cold. Pour dressing on top and serve.
Serves: 6

Sweet and Spicy Veggies

Ingredients:

2 c. butternut squash, frozen or fresh (peeled, seeded, and cut in one inch cubes)
3 c. sweet potatoes, frozen or fresh (peeled and cut in one inch cubes)
5 medium carrots, peeled and cut in one inch pieces
3 small onions, quartered
2 T. olive oil
2 T. honey
½ t. cumin
½ t. coriander
½ t. ginger
½ t. salt
¼ t. cayenne
¼ t. cinnamon

Place the raw vegetables into a large casserole dish. Mix the spices and salt in a small bowl or use a sealed container and shake well. Sprinkle the spices over the vegetables. Pour the honey over them. Mix well. Bake covered at 375° for 40 minutes and uncovered for 10 more minutes on the top rack to brown the vegetables. The vegetables should be tender. Test with a fork. Remove from the oven. Pour the olive oil on top and mix well before serving. Serves: 6-8 people

Sweet Potato Bake

Ingredients:

2 medium-large sweet potatoes, peeled and chopped in small chunks
3 sweet cooking apples, peeled and chopped in small chunks
3 large carrots, peeled and chopped in small chunks

Mix in a medium size casserole dish. Cover. Bake at 350° for 55 minutes. You should be able to easily put a fork in it when done.

Serves: 4-6

Tangy Bean Salad

Ingredients:

One 15-oz. can of great northern beans, or 2 c. of beans, fermented if preferred, and cooked and chilled
One 15-oz. can of chickpeas, or 2 c. of beans, fermented if preferred, and cooked and chilled
One 15-oz. can of kidney beans, or 2 c. of beans, fermented if preferred, and cooked and chilled
One small onion, finely chopped
1-2 stalks of celery, finely chopped
1½ T. dried parsley
⅓ c. apple cider vinegar
¼ c. honey
3 T. olive oil
1 t. salt

Add the first six ingredients to a large bowl and stir. Mix the last four ingredients in a small bowl. Stir well. Pour the mixture over the beans and stir until evenly distributed. Serve immediately or store in the refrigerator.
Serves: 6-8

Vegan Reuben Patties

Ingredients:

Patties
3 c. black beans, fermented if preferred, cooked (If using canned beans, you will need 2 cans and you will have some leftover.)

½ c. ground flax seed
3 t. sage
2 t. thyme
2 t. paprika
2 t. oregano
1 t. salt
1 t. black pepper
1 c. of sauerkraut, more or less as preferred
Thousand Island Dressing (See recipe in "Sauces and Dressings")

Place the beans and ⅓ cup of bean broth from the can or your cooking water in a high-powered blender. Blend until paste-like with some small bean chunks left. In a medium size bowl, mix all the spices, salt, and flax together or shake in a sealed container and pour into the bowl. Add the beans and stir with a spoon until thoroughly mixed. Using about two heaping tablespoonful's of the mixture, shape into equal size round patties. The patties will be about 2¼-2½ inches wide and ½ inch thick. Place on parchment paper in a glass pan. Bake at 350° for 20-23 minutes. They will come off clean when lifted off the paper. Place them on serving plates. Top with Thousand Island dressing and sauerkraut. If you would like a vegan Reuben sandwich, top two patties on toasted bread and serve.

Makes: 12-14 Reuben patties or 6-7 sandwiches

Tip: For Vegan Sausage patties: Follow the patty recipe and serve them plain without the dressing and sauerkraut. Serve them with our pancakes or breakfast burrito for a breakfast treat.

Desserts

Almond Butter Brownies

Ingredients:

Brownie Mixture:
1⅔ c. whole-wheat einkorn flour
2½ c. coconut sugar, unrefined
1¼ c. non-alkalized unsweetened cocoa powder
1 t. baking powder
1 t. salt
1 15-ounce can of black beans, drained or 2 c.
black beans, fermented if preferred, cooked, and
drained
1 t. vanilla extract
1⅔ c. water

Almond butter cookie topping:
½ c. whole-wheat einkorn flour
¼ c. coconut sugar, unrefined
½ t. baking powder
⅛ t. salt
⅓ c. raw almond butter (no added ingredients)
2 T. maple syrup
¾ t. vanilla

Put the first five ingredients of the brownie
mixture in a large bowl and mix well. Drain and
rinse the black beans. Put the beans and ⅔ cup of
water in a high-powered blender and puree. Add
the bean mixture, vanilla extract, and the
additional one-cup of water to the dry mixture
and mix with a spoon until well blended. Cut a
piece of parchment paper to fit the bottom of a
9X13 glass-baking dish. Place it on the bottom of

your dish. Add the brownie mixture and spread evenly into the pan. Set aside. While that is sitting, put the first four ingredients of the almond butter cookie topping into a medium size bowl and mix well. Add the almond butter, syrup, and vanilla extract and mix with a spoon until well blended. Form into small discs and place them approximately one quarter to one half inch apart in even rows on top of the brownie mixture. You may need to wet your hands when working with this sticky dough. Push the dough slightly down into the batter. The cookie dough should still be showing on top of the mixture. This will ensure the cookie mixture will disperse down into the brownies. Bake at 350° for 33-35 minutes until firm in the center and a toothpick in the center of the pan in the center of a cookie dough piece comes out clean. Let cool completely in the pan. Gently run a knife along the edges to loosen the sides before cutting into brownies. Store in an airtight container.

Almond Butter Cookies

Ingredients:

2 c. whole-wheat einkorn flour
1¼ c. raw almond butter (no added ingredients)
1 c. coconut sugar, unrefined
½ c. maple syrup
1 T. vanilla extract
2 t. baking powder
½ t. salt

Mix the flour, coconut sugar, baking powder, and salt together in a large bowl. Add the rest of the ingredients. Mix with a hand mixer until it forms dough. You can also knead with your hands at the end. This mixture will be slightly crumbly. Roll into 1½-inch balls. Then flatten them by molding and shaping them with your hands so they are about one-inch around. Place the cookies one inch apart on parchment paper on a baking sheet. Push a fork into some coconut sugar and lightly flatten the cookie again with the tines of a fork, forming a crisscross pattern. The cookie should now be about 1¼ inch around. Bake at 350° for 10 minutes. They will look slightly under cooked. Remove from oven and let sit for five minutes on the hot baking sheet. Using a spatula, remove them from the paper and let cool on paper towels. Store in airtight container.

Makes: 24 soft cookies

Almond Butter Cup Milkshake

Ingredients:

2 15-ounce cans of unsweetened full fat coconut milk
¼ c. and 3 T. of maple syrup
2 t. vanilla extract
3-4 almond butter cups (see recipe in "Desserts")

Place the milk in a high-powered blender and blend on low for one minute to mix the milk evenly. Set aside 1 cup of milk and store in the refrigerator. Using two ice cube trays, pour the remaining milk in to the trays. Freeze. Once completely frozen, use right away or seal in freezer bag to prevent freezer burn and ice build up. Chop up the almond butter cups into small pieces. Put the milk back in the high power blender. Add the syrup and vanilla and milk cubes. Gradually work up to high on your blender and blend for about one minute or until the milk cubes are smooth and have produced a milkshake consistency. Turn your blender off. Put the chopped almond butter cups into the mixture. Turn your machine on low until the cups are evenly mixed. Pour into glasses and enjoy.

Serves: 2-4 people depending on how big of a milkshake you desire.

Other flavors include:

- <u>Chocolate shake</u>: Add ⅔ c. of non-alkalized unsweetened cocoa powder to the unfrozen milk before adding the milk cubes. Increase the maple syrup to ½ cup and 2 tablespoons
- <u>Mint chocolate chip shake</u>: Add 1 t. peppermint extract and fold in 3 ounces of mini chocolate chips at the end
- <u>Strawberry shake</u>: Just use the plain vanilla based recipe above and add 3 cups of fresh strawberries or your favorite fruit

Note: You can use low fat coconut milk for this recipe but it does not taste as good and it is not as thick. Experiment what works for you.

Almond Butter Cups

Ingredients:

½ c. raw almond butter (no added ingredients)
3 T. and 2 t. coconut sugar, unrefined
1 T. and 2 t. maple syrup
½ t. vanilla extract
7 ounces of chocolate chips, melted
6 large unbleached baking cups

Mix the first four ingredients together in a small bowl. Shape into 6 even round balls. Set aside. Place baking cups in a muffin tin. Melt the chocolate in a double boiler pan. You can put a small pan in a medium pan of gently boiling water if you do not have a double boiler. Put approximately 1½ t. of melted chocolate on the bottom of the baking cups. Use a spoon and drag the chocolate up the side of the cups only about ⅛ of an inch. Put the tin in the freezer for about 5 minutes until the chocolate is firm and solid. Remove from the freezer. Flatten the nut butter balls to about ½ inch tall and so they are just slightly less smaller than the round chocolate bottom. Place the almond butter mix on top of the thin frozen chocolate bottom. Top with remaining melted chocolate in equal parts to cover and refreeze for 5-10 more minutes or until firm. You will have to use the spoon to let the chocolate fall to the sides of the nut butter mixture. Store in the refrigerator in a sealed container. Best when left out on the counter about 20 minutes before eating.

Makes: 6 large cups or 12 or more mini cups.

Tip: Sprinkle top with sea salt flakes before the final freeze if you want a salty sweet contrast.

Almond Crunch Fruit Whip

Ingredients:

Layer 1: Crust
2 c. chopped almonds, fermented and dried if preferred
2 T. maple syrup
½ t. salt

Layer 2: Strawberry Yogurt
1 c. cashews, fermented if preferred
12 oz. frozen strawberries
1 T. maple syrup
2 t. lemon juice
1 c. fresh strawberries, chopped

Layer 3: Cashew Cream
1 c. cashews, fermented if preferred
½ c. water
3 T. maple syrup
2 t. vanilla

Layer 4: Strawberry Syrup
6 oz. frozen strawberries
1 T. and 1½ t. maple syrup

<u>Layer 5</u>: Whipped Cream
1 15-ounce can unsweetened full fat coconut milk
(refrigerated for 24 hours, unopened)
1 T. maple syrup
1 t. vanilla

<u>Layer 1</u>: Chop nuts in a high-powered blender or food processor until small chunks are seen. Place in a medium baking dish. Add salt and syrup. Mix well. Cover and bake at 350° for 10 minutes. If fermenting, make sure your almonds are dried well before chopping. Remove from baking dish immediately and lay on parchment paper until it cools or it will stick to the dish. Place in sealed container on parchment paper until you are ready to use it. You may need to break the mixture up with a knife before serving.

<u>Layer2</u>: Place the first four ingredients in a high-powered blender. Blend until smooth. Place in a small bowl and gently stir in the fresh strawberries. Set aside.

<u>Layer 3</u>: Place all ingredients in a high-powered blender. Blend until smooth. Place in a small bowl. Set aside.

<u>Layer 4</u>: Place ingredients in a high-powered blender. Blend until smooth. Pour in a small bowl or container with a pour spout. Set aside.

<u>Layer 5</u>: Open the cold can of milk. Using a spoon, scoop out the thick solid white cream only. Place in a medium size bowl. Do not use any of the clear liquid, as this will make your whip cream runny. Discard the rest or save it if you can use it.

Add the syrup and vanilla. Blend with a hand mixer until it is light and fluffy.

Layers 2-5 can be refrigerated until you are ready to use. Store the almond mix in a tightly sealed container at room temperature.
When ready to serve, set aside four tablespoons of the almond mixture. Get four serving bowls and pour the remaining almond mixture into four equal parts on the bottom of the bowls. Layer the strawberry yogurt on top of the almond mixture in four equal portions. Repeat with the cashew cream, strawberry syrup, and whipped cream. Sprinkle one tablespoon of the reserved almond mixture on top of each serving bowl. Serve immediately.

Serves: 4 or more

Almost Heath Bar Cake

Ingredients:

Cake:
2 c. whole-wheat einkorn flour
½ c. non-alkalized unsweetened cocoa powder
1 c. coconut sugar, unrefined
2 T. ground flax seed
¾ t. baking powder
½ t. baking soda
⅓ c. honey
1⅓ c. water
½ c. avocado, pureed
1¼ t. vanilla extract
1¼ t. apple cider vinegar
1 c. mini chocolate chips

Mix the first six ingredients together in a large bowl. Blend the avocado and water in a high-powered blender until smooth. Add to the dry mixture along with the honey, vanilla extract, and apple cider vinegar. Stir with a spoon until it is thoroughly mixed. Fold in the chocolate chips. Cut a piece of parchment paper to line the bottom of an 8x8 glass-baking pan. Pour the batter evenly in the pan. Bake for 50-55 minutes at 350°. The cake may dip in the center and will slightly spring back when done. The sides of the cake will spring back more than the center will. Let cool at room temperature and prepare the rest of the layers in the order presented below.

Caramel
2 15-ounce cans of unsweetened full fat coconut
milk
½ c. and 2 T. maple syrup
2 t. vanilla extract
⅛ t. salt

Mix all of the ingredients together in a pan over
medium-high heat. Bring to a boil and stir
continuously without reducing the temperature.
Keep cooking until it thickens and starts to
darken. It will pour off your spoon like nectar
(slightly less thick than honey) when done.
Remove from heat. Set aside to cool. You can
store this in your refrigerator for up to one week.
Makes 1¼ cup of caramel and you will use the
whole amount for this cake.

Coconut Butter
7-8 ounce bag of shredded coconut

Pour the coconut in a high-powered blender.
Blend until smooth. This will make enough for
two plus cakes. Store in a jar or sealed container
in your pantry. This butter will last for a few
months.
Makes: ½ to ⅔ cup of butter

Vegan Sweetened Condensed Milk
¾ c. cashews, fermented if preferred
½ c. maple syrup
¼ c. coconut butter (see recipe above)
1 T. lemon juice (fresh juice is preferred)
2 t. vanilla extract

Make sure the ingredients are at room temperature. Place in high-powered blender. Blend until smooth. Pour into a jar or sealed container. This makes enough for one cake with some leftover. Set aside at room temperature to use for this cake. Store leftovers in a glass jar in the fridge and gently rewarm as needed.

Chocolate Caramel Crunch Topping
½ c. almonds, fermented and dried if preferred, chopped
¼ c. caramel, cooled (see recipe above)
⅓ c. mini chocolate chips

Place your almonds in a high-powered blender or food processor. A food processor works best for this. Chop until they produce small pieces but make sure they do not grind up fine. Mix all the ingredients in a small bowl. Line a cookie sheet with parchment paper. Using a spoon, scoop out the mixture onto the parchment paper. You will need to use your finger to slide the mixture off the spoon. Spread out in a thin layer. The mixture will not be even or smooth on your cookie sheet. Freeze for approximately 20 minutes or until you are ready to spread on the cake. This mixture will not completely firm up.

Whipped Cream
1 15-ounce can full fat coconut milk (refrigerated for 24 hours, unopened)
1 T. maple syrup
1 t. vanilla extract

Open the cold can of milk. Using a spoon, scoop out the thick solid white cream. Place in a medium size bowl. Do not use any of the clear liquid, as this will make your whip cream runny. Discard the rest or save it if you can use it. Add the syrup and vanilla. Blend with a hand mixer until it is light and fluffy. Refrigerate until ready to use.

Using your beater from a hand mixer without the collar (the lip that allows it to lock into the larger hole), turn it on end (beater side up) and punch holes in the cake in even rows one inch apart. Continue this on the entire cake. Mix one cup of cooled caramel and one cup of vegan sweetened condensed milk in a medium size bowl. Mix thoroughly. Pour over the entire cake. Make sure the cake is cool. Refrigerate for 30 minutes. Add the whipped cream and spread evenly over the entire cake. Using a spoon, scoop up pieces of the chocolate caramel crunch topping. Drop in small dollops on top of the whipped topping and disperse evenly. This final topping will cover most of the cake. Cut and serve immediately or refrigerate until ready to serve. As you slice and serve this cake, the topping will run all over the sides. It is a gooey mess but that is the design of this yummy cake. Refrigerate leftovers. Best if eaten in three days.

Banana Chip Muffins

Ingredients:

1½ c. whole-wheat einkorn flour
¾ c. coconut sugar, unrefined
2 t. baking powder
½ t. baking soda
¼ t. salt
1 t. cinnamon
1 c. bananas, mashed with a fork
2 T. unsweetened almond milk
½ c. egg replacer
½ c. mini chocolate chips
14 large unbleached baking cups

Mix the dry ingredients in a large bowl. Add the bananas, milk, and egg replacer. Blend with a hand mixer until well blended. Fold in the chocolate chips. Place batter in the baking cups in a muffin tin ¾ of the way to the top. Bake at 400° for 20 minutes or until a toothpick comes out clean in the center. Cool completely and refrigerate. Remove from the refrigerator and gently peel the wrapper off immediately. If you peel them at room temperature, the wrapper will stick.

Makes: 12-14 muffins

Carrot Cake Cookies

Ingredients:
1 c. whole-wheat einkorn flour

1 c. carrots, grated
½ c. raisins
½ c. walnuts, finely chopped
½ c. unsweetened coconut, shredded
½ c. maple syrup
1 t. baking powder
1 T. cinnamon
1 t. nutmeg
½ t. ginger
2 t. vanilla extract

Cinnamon Glaze
¼ c. virgin coconut oil that is hexane free, room temperature
1 t. vanilla
2 T. maple syrup
1 t. cinnamon

Mix the flour, baking powder, and spices in a medium bowl. Add the rest of the cookie ingredients and stir until blended well. Place approximately two tablespoons of dough in a rounded spoonful on parchment paper on a baking sheet. Bake at 350° for 20 minutes. Let cool for several minutes before lifting off of the parchment paper. These come off very easily. Meanwhile, place all of the glaze ingredients in a small bowl. Mix with a hand mixer until evenly blended. The blending rod or a puree attachment tool works best. You may have to re-blend right before spreading. Spread in equal parts on top of completely cooled cookies.
Makes: 12-14 cookies

Tip: For a healthier version, exclude the glaze.

Creamy Berry Delight

Ingredients:

½ c. of blueberries
½ c. blackberries
½ c. strawberries, chopped
½ c. pineapple, chopped
½ c. walnuts, chopped

Cashew Cream
1 c. cashews, fermented if preferred
½ c. water
3 T. maple syrup
2 t. vanilla

Place the cashew cream ingredients in a high-powered blender. Blend until smooth. Transfer to a medium size-serving bowl. Add the fruit and walnuts to the cream. Mix well. Chill and serve.

Serves: 4

Orange Creamsicles

Ingredients:

1 c. fresh squeezed orange juice
1 c. unsweetened almond milk
4 t. honey
1 t. orange extract
1 t. vanilla extract

Blend in a blender on low to mix the honey through. Pour into your popsicle molds and freeze immediately.

Makes approximately 4 popsicles depending on the size of your molds.

Raw Key Lime Pie

Ingredients:

Crust:
1 c. walnuts, fermented and dried if preferred
1 c. almonds, fermented and dried if preferred
1 c. pecans, fermented and dried if preferred
2 oz. dates, pitted
1 T. maple syrup
1 t. vanilla extract

Filling:
2 c. cashews
8 oz. fresh avocado, peeled and de-pitted
¾ c. fresh squeezed lime juice (about 3-4 good size limes)
¾ c. maple syrup
1 t. vanilla extract

Whipped Cream Topping:(this is a slightly different version from our regular recipe)
One 15-ounce can of full fat unsweetened coconut milk (refrigerated for 24 hours, unopened)
2 T. maple syrup
1 t. vanilla extract

Place the crust ingredients in a high-powered blender or food processor. Blend until a crumbly crust consistency. There will be some small nut pieces but it will almost be dough-like. The food processor works best with this but if you do not have one, you may have to do the nuts in stages depending on your blender type. Just pour the blended mixture in a medium size bowl to hand mix everything together a final time. Press the mixture on the bottom of a 9-inch pie plate. Place in the refrigerator while you make the filling. Place the filling ingredients in a high-powered blender. When the filling is completely smooth and creamy, scoop out in to a medium glass bowl. Place in the freezer to cool the mixture, as it will be a little warm from blending. After about 10 minutes or so the filling should be cool to the touch. Using a spoon, scoop out the filling into the piecrust. Freeze for one hour. Meanwhile, make the whipping cream. Open the cold can of milk. Using a spoon, scoop out the thick solid white cream only. Place in a medium size bowl. Do not use any of the clear liquid, as this will make your whip cream runny. Discard the rest or save it if you can use it. Add the syrup and vanilla. Blend with a hand mixer until it is light and fluffy. Refrigerate until ready to use. After one hour, remove the pie from the freezer and cut. Top with whipped cream. Serve and refrigerate leftovers. The pie is best if consumed in two days.

Raw Lava Cake

Ingredients:

Cake:
1½ c. walnuts, fermented and patted dry if
preferred
2 ounces of dates, pitted
½ c. raisins
⅓ c. non-alkalized unsweetened cocoa powder or
carob powder (raw is best)
1 t. vanilla extract
⅛ t. salt

Lava Sauce:
¼ c. maple syrup
2 T. non-alkalized unsweetened cocoa powder or
carob powder (raw is best)
* If you used cocoa for the cake, use cocoa for the
sauce and vise versa.

Blend all the cake ingredients in a high-powered
blender or food processor. The food processor
works best with this if you have one. Blend until
the food begins to stick together and appears
crumbly. You may see tiny pieces of raisins left
but the ingredients will be mostly ground up
smooth. Place in a bowl and divide into 6 equal
portions. Work with each one like play-dough
until the mixture is warm, soft, and pliable. Shape
into a small bowl by sticking your thumb in the
center and forming the sides. This will produce
your small bowl shape cake with a hole in the
center. Place each cake on separate serving

plates. In a small bowl, mix the lava sauce ingredients with a spoon until a smooth consistency is formed. Pour in equal portions in the center to overflow in each cake. Serve cakes immediately or store in a sealed container in the fridge for later. Just set out the cakes to warm to room temperature before serving and do not add the sauce until you serve. Re-stir the lava sauce before pouring.

Makes: 6 lava cakes

Tip: The carob is harder to work with when forming the cake. It is a bit more crumbly so just work with it more than the cocoa. It is super delicious however and a healthier version of this yummy lava cake.

Raw Vanilla Chocolate Surprise Cheesecake

Ingredients:

Crust:
1½ c. walnuts, fermented if preferred
1½ c. pecans, fermented if preferred
¼ c. non-alkalized unsweetened cocoa powder
3 ounces dates, pitted
¼ c. maple syrup
1 t. vanilla extract

Vanilla Filling:
3 c. cashews, fermented if preferred
½ c. maple syrup

¼ c. lemon juice from fresh lemons (about 2 medium)
1 T. vanilla extract
⅛ t. salt

Chocolate filling and topping:
½ c. non-alkalized unsweetened cocoa powder
¾ c. maple syrup
2 T. raw almond butter (no added ingredients)

Place the crust ingredients in a high-powered blender or food processor. Blend until a dough-like consistency. There will be some small nut pieces in the mix. The food processor works best with this but if you do not have one, you may have to do the mixture in stages depending on your blender type. Just pour the blended mixture in a medium size bowl to hand mix everything together a final time. Press the mixture on the bottom of a 9-inch pie plate. Place in the freezer while you make the vanilla filling. Place the vanilla filling ingredients in a high-powered blender. When the filling is completely smooth and creamy, scoop out in to a medium glass bowl. Remove the pie shell from the freezer and place half of the vanilla filling in the shell. Spread the filling evenly. Place it back in the freezer for 30 minutes or until firm to the touch. Keep the remaining vanilla filling at room temperature. Meanwhile, place the chocolate filling and topping ingredients in a small bowl. Mix with a hand mixer until evenly blended. The blending rod or a puree attachment tool works best. When the chocolate is blended, set aside ¼ cup of the chocolate filling for the topping. Keep the chocolate filling and the chocolate topping out at room temperature. When the 30 minutes are up, take the cake out of the freezer. Spread the chocolate filling (this is the larger amount) over the frozen vanilla filling. Make sure it is even and smooth, being careful not to puncture the vanilla layer (it is fine if you do as this will not ruin the cake). Return to the freezer for one hour until this layer is firm. Please note that this layer will not be as firm and solid as the vanilla layer but the desired outcome is to have it firm enough to spread the last layer on top without the layers mixing. Once the chocolate filling is firm, spread the remaining vanilla filling over top of the chocolate layer. Make sure to spread it gently again. Pour the chocolate topping in small trails or rows across the entire cake. With a light touch, drag a knife or toothpick back and forth perpendicularly to the lines you made. This makes a marbled type effect. Return to the freezer again for one hour. This cake can then be cut right away and eaten. A fully frozen cake that has been frozen all-day or overnight will need to sit out for about 25-40 minutes before slicing. We have found that this varies greatly depending on the time of year and the temperature of your house. You should be able to slice it fairly easily with a knife. Do not let it warm up too much though. You may have to gently loosen the crust edges with your serving utensil first before sliding the utensil down to remove the cake. This cake comes out very easily. It is best eaten when the vanilla is soft enough to put a fork down through it but still remains cold. Cover with saran wrap and refreeze any leftovers.

Pineapple Fluff

Ingredients:

One 20 oz. can of pineapple chunks, drained and cut into small pieces, or you can use fresh pineapple if desired

Almond Crunch
2 c. chopped almonds, fermented and dried if preferred
2 T. maple syrup
½ t. salt

Chop nuts in a high-powered blender or food processor until small chunks are seen. Place in a medium baking dish. Add salt and syrup. Mix well. Cover and bake at 350° for 10 minutes. If fermenting, make sure your almonds are dried well before chopping. To prevent sticking, remove from baking dish immediately and lay on parchment paper until it cools. Place in sealed container on parchment paper until you are ready to use it. You may need to break the mixture up with a knife before serving.

Cashew Cream
2 c. cashews, fermented if preferred
1 c. water
¼ c. and 2 T. maple syrup
4 t. vanilla

Place the cashew cream ingredients in high-powered blender. Blend until smooth. Set aside.

Whipping Cream
1 15-ounce can of unsweetened full fat coconut milk (refrigerated for 24 hours, unopened)
1 T. maple syrup
1 t. vanilla

Open the cold can of milk. Using a spoon, scoop out the thick solid white cream only. Place in a medium size bowl. Do not use any of the clear liquid, as this will make your whip cream runny. Discard the rest or save it if you can use it. Add the syrup and vanilla. Blend with a hand mixer until it is light and fluffy.

Place the pineapple, almond crunch, and cashew cream in a bowl and fold in until well mixed. Spoon into serving bowls and top with whipped cream. Serve immediately.

Serves: 4

Tip: This tastes best fresh so the almond crunch does not soften. You can keep layers separate in the fridge until ready to mix and serve.

Tip: Crushed pineapple does not have a good flavor in this recipe.

Strawberry Orange Chocolate Chip Scones with Vanilla Orange Glaze

Ingredients:

<u>Scone</u>
2 c. whole-wheat einkorn flour
⅓ c. coconut sugar, unrefined
1 T. baking powder
¼ c. mini chocolate chips
½ c. unsweetened almond milk
1 t. vanilla extract
1 t. orange extract
1 c. fresh strawberries, finely chopped

<u>Topping:</u> Pick one of the two options listed below

Use the glaze or cream. The glaze is our favorite but with the use of coconut oil, it is a less healthy option. We use this only for an occasional treat.

Using the scone ingredients, in a medium or large bowl, mix flour, baking powder, and sugar. In a small bowl, mix milk, vanilla, and orange. Add the wet and dry ingredients together and stir with a spoon. When it forms a dough, hand mix to form a dough ball. Add the chocolate chips and strawberries and mix well. This will not mix in easy. You need to push or press in the ingredients a bit for the chips and berries to disperse through the dough. Use a floured pastry sheet or a floured counter surface and rolling pin to roll out the dough to a 10-inch circle. Using a pizza cutter cut 8 equal triangle slices. Place parchment paper on a cooking sheet to completely cover. Place the sliced scones on the paper. Bake at 400° for 15 minutes. Remove and cool.

1. Glaze
¼ c. virgin coconut oil that is hexane free, room temperature
1 t. vanilla
2 T. maple syrup
1 t. of orange oil extract or more to taste

Place all of the glaze ingredients in a small bowl. Mix with a hand mixer until evenly blended. The blending rod or a puree attachment tool works best. You may have to re-blend right before spreading. Spread in equal parts on top of completely cooled scones.

2. Cream
One 15-ounce can of unsweetened full fat coconut milk (refrigerated for 24 hours, unopened)
1 t. vanilla
2 T. maple syrup
1 t. of orange oil extract or more to taste

Open the cold can of milk. Using a spoon, scoop out the thick solid white cream only. Place in a medium size bowl. Do not use any of the clear liquid, as this will make your whip cream runny. Discard the rest or save it if you can use it. Add the syrup, orange, and vanilla. Blend with a hand mixer until it is light and fluffy. Spoon some cream on your plate and top some cream on each bite.
Makes 8 scones

Snacks

Chicki-Pops

Ingredients:

2 15-ounce cans of chickpeas or 4 c. chickpeas, fermented if preferred and cooked
¼ c. olive oil
1 T. paprika
1 T. cumin
¼ t. cayenne
1 t. salt

Pat dry your chickpeas with paper towels to eliminate excess water. Mix all of the seasonings together in a small sealed container by shaking it. Put the chickpeas and seasonings in a bowl and mix to coat. Add the oil and mix again. Pour them into your glass baking dishes (you will need more than one). Make sure they are in a single layer in your baking dish. Roast them in your oven at 170° for 6-8 hours depending on the amount of crunchiness you prefer. Six hours is a softer snack. Eight hours may be too crunchy for some. Try taking some chicki-pops out after 6, 7 and 8 hours and adjust your roasting time in the future to the optimal roasting time for you. Let cool and place in a storage container.

Tip: We love to use this as a movie snack and a substitution for popcorn.

Serves: 4

Trail Mix

Ingredients:

1½ c. chicki-pops (see recipe in "Snacks")
1 c. spiced pecans (see directions below)
½ c. raw almonds, fermented and dried if
preferred
⅓ c. raw pumpkin seeds, fermented and dried if
preferred
⅓ c. raw sunflower seeds, fermented and dried if
preferred
⅓ c. raisins
¼-½ t. salt

Spiced Pecans:
1 c. pecans, fermented if preferred
1 t. cinnamon
1 t. vanilla extract
2 t. maple syrup

In a small bowl, add maple syrup, cinnamon, and
vanilla. Mix well. Add the pecans on top and mix
well. Place in a glass pan in a single layer and
bake at 170° stirring occasionally until they begin
to dry and the mixture crystalizes on the nuts,
about 20 minutes. Set aside. If you do not
ferment, the baking time will be shorter. Watch
that you do not burn the nuts. Let cool.

Place the almonds, pumpkin seeds, and sunflower
seeds in a sealed container with salt. Shake well.
The amount of salt will vary depending on your
taste preference and if you fermented your nuts

and seeds. Fermentation of nuts and seeds requires salt and so they will naturally be saltier to begin with. Try ¼ teaspoon, taste them, and add more if needed. If you bought salted nuts and seeds already, skip this step. Pour the salted almonds and seeds in a medium size bowl. Add the chicki-pops, spiced pecans, and raisins. Mix well. Store in a sealed container at room temperature or in the refrigerator. If you fermented your snack ingredients, it spoils sooner. Best if eaten in one week.

Makes: 4 cups

Breads

Croutons

Ingredients:

2 c. einkorn bread, cubed
3 T. olive oil
1½ t. onion granules
1½ t. garlic granules
1 t. basil
1 t. parsley
½ t. thyme
½ t. sage
¼ t. dry mustard
½ t. salt
Two large pinches of cayenne

Mix the dry herbs together in a small bowl. Add the olive oil to the herbs and mix well. Place the bread in a glass-baking dish. Pour the oil mixture over the bread and mix well making sure all bread is coated. Place the seasoned breadcrumbs in a single layer. Bake at 170° for approximately 3 hours, mixing half way through. Your croutons should be crunchy but not burnt. Let cool and use for salads. These are best if used within a day or two.

Oil Free Tortilla Wraps

Ingredients:

2 c. whole-wheat einkorn flour
¾ c. unsweetened almond milk
½ t. salt
¾ t. onion granules
¾ t. garlic granules
½ t. parsley
¼ t. basil
¼ t. oregano
⅛ t. thyme

Mix the dry ingredients in a medium bowl. Add the milk. Mix with a spoon and then begin to knead with your hands for about three minutes, until well mixed. Put a light dusting of flour over the dough. Place the dough back in the bowl and cover with a towel in a dark place and let it rest for 30 minutes. Divide into 12 balls. Roll out the dough on a heavily floured surface on top and bottom. Roll into ⅛ inch thick circles. Heat a skillet on medium heat. Do not use oil. Place the wrap in the hot, dry skillet until it starts bubbling up underneath, about 30-60 seconds. Flip for 30 more seconds. About halfway through making all your tortilla wraps, the flour in the skillet will start blackening. Some of this flour will get on your wraps, but it is perfectly fine and does not alter the taste. Store in a sealed container if you do not use them right away. Best if eaten within a few days.

Makes: 12 small wraps

Tip: If you prefer to fry your wraps and roll them out on a greased surface, feel free to do so. This oil free recipe however is healthier and tastes great.

Whole Wheat Einkorn Biscuits

Ingredients:

2½ c. whole-wheat einkorn flour
3 t. baking powder
½ t. salt
1 T. honey
¾ c. unsweetened almond milk plus an additional amount to cover the biscuit tops
2 T. pureed applesauce

Mix the dry ingredients together in a medium bowl. Add the milk, applesauce, and honey. Stir with a spoon, and then knead well until thoroughly mixed. Shape into 8 round biscuits and place on parchment paper in covered casserole dishes. Using a small spoon, pour a small amount of almond milk on the top of each biscuit. Make sure the entire top is wet. Bake covered at 350° for 20 minutes. Serve warm.

Makes: 8 biscuits

Tip: These are good with our soups.

Whole Wheat Einkorn Bread

Ingredients:

3¾ c. whole-wheat einkorn flour
1¼ c. warm water
4 t. baking powder
1 T. honey

Mix the dry ingredients so it is evenly distributed. Add the honey and water. Mix with a spoon and then begin to knead with your hands for about three minutes, until well mixed. If you have a mixer, use it according to your instructions. Pat and shape into a loaf. Dust the dough with flour. Place in a loaf pan, lined with a strip of parchment paper to cover the bottom. It is fine if the paper goes up the sides a little bit. Cover with a towel. Place in a warm enclosed place for 30 minutes such as a toaster oven on warm or an oven slightly warmed and turned off. After 30 minutes, remove the towel. Bake at 350° for 30 minutes. Remove from loaf pan. Use a knife to loosen the sides if needed. This pops out very easily without sticking. Peel the parchment paper off the bottom. Cool before slicing. This bread will rise but not as well as if you are using yeast. We find this healthier yeast-free bread rises sufficient enough for a nice loaf, if you follow these directions.

Sauces & Dressings

Barbeque Sauce

Ingredients:

1 15-ounce can of tomato sauce
⅓ c. apple cider vinegar
⅓ c. honey
1 6-ounce can of tomato paste
½ c. black strap molasses
3 T. coconut aminos
1 t. paprika
1 t. garlic granules
½ t. black pepper
½ t. onion granules
½ t. salt
A few pinches of cayenne

Place the ingredients in a medium pan and mix together. Bring to a boil over medium heat. Reduce to low and simmer uncovered for 20 minutes or until thickened, stirring occasionally. Cool and refrigerate and use as needed.

Makes: 3 cups

Tip: Freeze in ½ c. portions for buffalo bites or quantity desired for other recipes.

Honey Mustard Dressing

Ingredients:

¼ c. of honey
2 T. vegenaise
3 T. yellow mustard
2 T. apple cider vinegar
2 T. olive oil
⅛ t. salt
Dash of black pepper

Put all ingredients in a salad dressing container.
Close and shake well. Refrigerate. Use within one
week.

Makes: ¾ cup of dressing

Italian Dressing

Ingredients:

¼ c. apple cider vinegar
½ c. olive oil
1½ t. onion granules
¾ t. garlic granules
1 t. oregano
1 t. basil
1 t. parsley
½ t. salt
½ t. black pepper
¼ t. thyme
¼ t. celery seed

Put all ingredients in a salad dressing container. Close and shake well or stir. You can store in a dark place for a few days or store in the refrigerator for 1-2 weeks. Remember that fresh is best.

Makes: ¾ cup of dressing

Poppy seed Dressing

Ingredients:

3 T. vegenaise
2 T. olive oil
1½ t. apple cider vinegar
2 t. honey
2 T. almond milk
½ t. poppy seeds
1 t. onion granules
¼ t. garlic granules
¼ t. dry mustard
Pinch of salt and pepper

Put all ingredients in a salad dressing container.
Close and shake well. Refrigerate. Use within one
week.

Makes: ½ cup of dressing

Ranch Dressing

Ingredients:

1 c. vegenaise
4 t. apple cider vinegar
4 t. almond milk
1 t. garlic granules
2 t. onion granules
2 t. chives
2 t. parsley
2 t. dill
½ t. dry mustard
¼ t. salt

Place ingredients in a small bowl and stir well.
Pour into salad dressing container. Shake before
serving. Refrigerate. Use within one week.
Makes: 1⅛ cup of dressing

Thousand Island Dressing

Ingredients:

1 c. vegenaise
¼ c. ketchup
2 T. bread and butter pickles, finely chopped
1 t. onion, finely chopped
1 small garlic clove, minced

Place all ingredients in your salad dressing
container. Mix well. Refrigerate. Mix before
serving. Use within one week.
Makes: 1¼ cup

Seasonings & Miscellaneous

Baking Powder

Ingredients:

2 T. baking soda
¼ c. cream of tartar
2 T. arrowroot powder

Sift all the ingredients together. Store in an airtight container.

Makes: ½ cup

Cashew Cheese

Ingredients:

1 c. cashews, fermented if you choose
⅓ c. water
¼ t garlic granules
1 t. onion powder
1 t. lemon juice
1 t. salt

Blend in a high-powered blender until smooth.

Egg Replacer

Ingredients:

1½ c. water
½ c. ground flax seed

Blend in a high-powered blender for two minutes. Chill for one hour before using. We have found however that it is still effective if used before chilling. Store leftover in fridge for up to one week.

¼ c. egg replacer = 1 egg

Spaghetti Squash Pasta

One large spaghetti squash will serve four people. Bake according to directions and slice in half. Remove seeds. With a fork, scrape in downward strokes to shred the squash and it will come out in strings like spaghetti noodles. Serve warm over your favorite pasta dish recipe.

Taco Seasoning

Ingredients:

½ c. chili powder
¼ c. onion granules
⅛ c. cumin
1 T. garlic granules
1 T. paprika
1 T. salt

Put in a sealed container and shake well. Store.

Whipped Cream

Ingredients:

1 15-ounce can full fat coconut milk (refrigerated for 24 hours, unopened)
1 T. maple syrup
1 t. vanilla extract

Open the cold can of milk. Using a spoon, scoop out the thick solid white cream only. Place in a medium size bowl. Do not use any of the clear liquid, as this will make your whip cream runny. Discard the rest or save it if you can use it. Add the syrup and vanilla. Blend with a hand mixer until it is light and fluffy. Serve immediately.

Zucchini Pasta

Use enough zucchini for the amount of people you want to serve. Wash your zucchini and keep the skin on. Use a spiralizer or vegetable peeler to make your zucchini noodles. Place zucchini in a bowl and sprinkle with ¼ teaspoon salt. Let it sit for 30 minutes. Drain the water and serve as your pasta.